THE BRAWLER'S ENCYCLOPEDIA

THE BRAWLER'S ENCYCLOPEDIA

AN UNOFFICIAL STRATEGY GUIDE FOR PLAYERS OF BRAWL STARS

JASON R. RICH

Sky Pony Press
New York

Sky Pony Press books may be purchased in bulk at special discounts for sales promotion, corporate gifts, fund-raising, or educational purposes. Special editions can also be created to specifications. For details, contact the Special Sales Department, Sky Pony Press, 307 West 36th Street, 11th Floor, New York, NY 10018 or info@skyhorsepublishing.com.

Sky Pony® is a registered trademark of Skyhorse Publishing, Inc.®, a Delaware corporation.

Visit our website at www.skyponypress.com.

10 9 8 7 6 5 4 3 2

Library of Congress Cataloging-in-Publication Data is available on file.

Series design by Brian Peterson

Hardcover ISBN: 978-1-5107-5517-8
E-book ISBN: 978-1-5107-5748-6

Printed in China

TABLE OF CONTENTS

Section 1—Let's Get Brawling....................1

Overview of *Brawl Stars* 7

Each Brawler is Unique.........................8

Discover Your Main Objectives 10

Popular Types of Events 14

Collecting and Using Coins, Gems,
   Tokens, Power Points, and Star Points 20

Do You Have What It Takes to Earn
   the "Star Player" Title?....................24

Know When to Rush, Hide, Take Cover,
   or Retreat.................................25

**Section 2—How to Download the Game
   and Get Started**..........................27

Is Playing *Brawl Stars* Really Free?............29

Minimum Mobile Device Requirements 29

How to Download *Brawl Stars* on the
   iPhone or iPad 29

Brawl Stars May Support a Controller
   When Running iOS 13.....................30

How to Download and Install *Brawl Stars*
   on an Android-Based Mobile Device 30

Play *Brawl Stars* on a Windows PC or Mac 34

   How to Install and Play *Brawl Stars*
      on your Windows PC or Mac............34

Adjusting the *Brawl Stars* Game Settings 36

Take Advantage of Supercell ID to Protect
   Your Account 38

Section 3—Meet the Brawlers 41

Discover Each Brawler's Unique Skills
   and Capabilities...........................43

   Health 43

   Attack 45

   Super 45

   Star Power 46

   How to Upgrade Your Brawlers............46

Get to Know the Brawlers....................47

   Barley....................................48

Bibi......................................50

Bo 52

Brock 53

Bull 55

Carl 57

Colt......................................58

Crow.................................... 60

Darryl 62

Dynamike 64

El Primo 65

Frank 67

Gene....................................68

Jessie....................................70

Leon 72

Mortis 73

Nita.....................................75

Pam.....................................77

Penny 79

Piper.................................... 81

Poco 82

Rico.....................................84

Rosa 86

Shelly 88

Spike 90

Tara 92

Tick......................................94

More Brawlers Are Always On the Way 95

What to Expect From New Brawlers 96

Unlock Brawler Skins and Upgrade Your
   Brawlers.................................96

**Section 4—35 Brawl Star Strategies
   for Newbs**.................................. 99

#1—There Are Two Ways to Practice
   Your Brawling Skills 101

Test Your Brawling Skills in the
   Training Cave...........................101

Consider Participating in a Friendly
   Game...................................103

#2—Create Your Three-Brawler Team 105
    Brawler Power Level Upgrade Chart 106
#3—Use Gems to Buy a Token Doubler 107
#4—Use Your Attack (Ammo) Wisely 108
#5—Don't Walk in a Straight Line 108
#6—Heal Up Before Your Next Attack 108
#7—Always Check the Bushes 109
#8—Look for Choke Points in Each Arena 110
#9—Every Brawler's Attack Has a Range
    and a Spread 110
#10—Choose Your Brawler Based
    on the Event and Arena 111
#11—Be Prepared to Defend Your Teammates
    Even If Your Brawler Might Perish 111
#12—Look for Arrow Tiles on the Floor
    of Some Arenas 112
#13—Don't Get Boxed In By Water 112
#14—Understand the Difference Between
    Power Level and Rank 113
#15—Unlock and Experience Multiple
    Events Each Day 113
#16—Use the Solo Showdown Event
    to Gain Trophies 114
#17—Peek Out from Behind Walls to Lure
    Your Enemies 115
#18—Move In to Attack and Then Quickly
    Retreat 115
#19—Learn to Dance 116
#20—Gang Up On One Enemy 116
#21—Attack the Enemy's Respawn Area 116
#22—Work with Teammates and Bait
    Your Enemies 117
#23—Sneak Up From Behind 117
#24—Keep Opening Boxes 117
#25—Ticketed Events Usually Offer the
    Best Prizes 119
#26—Learn to Dodge Incoming Attacks 120
#27—Don't Stay Too Close to Your
    Teammates 120
#28—Be Smart When Using Your Brawler's
    Super Capability 121

#29—Protect Your Stars or Gems 121
#30—Keep Your Team's Healer In the
    Middle 121
#31—Screenshot and Print the Arena Maps . . . 121
    A Selection of Arena Layouts 122
#32—Blast Away Solid Barriers When
    Necessary 123
#33—Avoid the Toxic Green Clouds 123
#34—Choose Any Event and Arena Map
    When Playing a Friendly Game 124
#35—Support Your Teammates in Gem Grab 124

Section 5—What's Offered From the Shop 125
Check Out the Daily Deals 127
How to Upgrade a Brawler Using
    Power Points 128
Big Boxes and Mega Boxes Can Be
    Purchased As Well 129
Skins Can Be Purchased Using Star Points 130
Consider Purchasing a Token Doubler 130
The Shop Sells Gem Packs 130
The Price of Gem Packs 130
Use Gems to Purchase Coin Bundles 131
Quit Shopping and Start Brawling 131
Redeem Prizes from Trophy Road 131

Section 6—Join Some Online Clubs and Chat . . . 133
How to Choose Your Name 135
How to Change Your Name 135
Linking with Facebook 135
Use LINE Connect to Link with Online
    Friends 136
Participate in *Brawl Stars* Clubs 137
Participate in Team Chats 139
Chat with Online Players .139

Section 7—*Brawl Stars* Online Resources 141
Your Brawling Excitement and Challenges
    Continue 146

SECTION 1

LET'S GET BRAWLING

Get ready to experience an action-oriented, multi-player shootout that's become mega-popular everywhere in the world where mobile games are played.

Brawl Stars was developed by a mobile app developer called Supercell (www.supercell.com). Like any well-designed game, this one is relatively easy to learn, yet extremely difficult to master. If you've already played games like *Clash Royale*, *Boom Beach*, *Clash of Clans*, or *Hay Day* on your mobile device, you already know that Supercell publishes some

truly clutch games. ***Brawl Stars*** is no exception! In fact, many gamers believe this is Supercell's most lit game yet.

You'll quickly discover that playing ***Brawl Stars*** requires fast thinking, even faster reflexes, and the need to continuously utilize creative strategies to outsmart your adversaries.

Just when you start getting really good at one of **Brawl Stars**'s popular game play modes (Events), you can switch to a different one. Each offers a unique set of challenges.

Another way to change up your gaming experience is to select a different brawler (character). Each requires you to master a different set of fighting techniques and gaming strategies.

What's great about **Brawl Stars** is that it can be played almost anytime and anywhere on your Internet-connected smartphone or tablet. Each individual match lasts just a few minutes. Yet you can easily spend several hours at a time working with any of the different brawlers as you try to boost their level and consistently achieve victories during brawls. The Solo Showdown Event shown here is being experienced on an iPhone.

Shown here is a match being played on an iPad. As you can see, the game screen is very similar to how the action appears on an iPhone or Android-based mobile device.

While some of the Events featured in **Brawl Stars** require you to compete against "bots," which are computer-controlled opponents, the majority of the different Events (like Gem Grab, Showdown, Heist, Bounty, or Brawl Ball) allow you to experience the real-time, multi-player action that makes this game so special.

At the start of each match, choose one brawler to control. Initially, when you start playing **Brawl Stars**, only one brawler will be unlocked and available. Once you start achieving victories, you'll be able to unlock additional brawlers, boost the level of each brawler available to you, and then customize each brawler's appearance using skins. Some brawlers can only be unlocked by making

in-app purchases as you progress through the game. These cost real money but are optional.

Depending on which game play mode (Event) you select, you'll compete alone against a small army of other brawlers (each of whom is being controlled by another gamer in real time), or you'll be teamed up with other gamers (each controlling their own brawler). When you have a partner or team, working together to defeat the opposing brawlers is often essential.

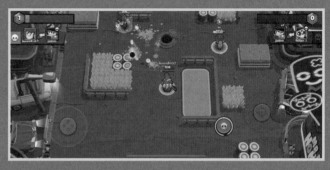

Gem Grab—the most popular Event in **Brawl Stars**—allows you to join a team of three brawlers in a fast-paced, 3 vs 3 scramble. The goal is to find and collect purple gems while fighting against the opposing team. When playing Gem Grab, the first three-person team to grab and hold onto 10 gems for a total of 15 seconds wins that match. Sounds easy, right? Well, it's not!

Each brawler has their own unique skill set and fighting capabilities. For example, in addition to a brawler's Health meter (a measure of how much damage they can take before being defeated), each has a unique Attack, Super, and Star Power capability that can be used in battle. Your goal as a gamer is to continuously improve the Rank and Power Level of the brawler you're working with, plus progress through the game and increase your level as a gamer by collecting and winning Trophies.

Each Event takes place in an arena. Each arena offers a unique layout. For example, once you choose to participate in a Gem Grab Event, each match can take place in one of more than 15 different arenas. When playing a 3 vs 3 match, it's essential to work together with your teammates, know how to best control your own brawler, and make the best use of your surroundings (based on the arena you're in).

As you'll discover shortly by reading this unofficial guide, it's best to assign a specific role to each teammate when playing certain types of Events. Remember, when playing Gem Grab, for example, collecting and holding onto the gems is essential, but defeating your enemies and defending yourself and your teammates is equally important.

Brawl Stars is continuously evolving. As of early summer 2019, the game featured 27 different brawlers. However, additional brawler characters, brawler skins (and capabilities), arenas, and types of Events are constantly being introduced into the game, so there's always something new to experience and new challenges to overcome. To discover what's new in the game, from the game's Home screen (shown here), tap the News icon. It's located on the left-side of the screen.

From the News screen, learn all about the latest game updates, new brawlers, new game play modes, new brawler skins, and what new Events have recently been added to the game by Supercell.

As part of this game update, a set of Retropolis skins for a variety of different brawlers was added to the game.

By making purchases from the Shop, you're able to unlock and acquire skins. These are used to customize the appearance of your favorite brawlers. Shown here is the Bandita Shelly skin for Shelly. To unlock it, the cost is 30 Gems (approximately $1.99 US), but you can preview this skin by tapping the Try button. In some cases, skins can be purchased (with real money) from the Shop.

Overview of *Brawl Stars*

Brawl Stars is all about brawling (combat). You need to outfight and outsmart your enemies, and achieve specific objectives during each match, often while racing against a countdown timer.

Sometimes you'll be working alone, such as when you experience a Solo Showdown Event. Most of the time, however, you'll be working with a partner, or as part of a multi-brawler team (shown here).

For the Events where your brawler has a partner or team, you can choose the other gamers you'll work with from your online friends or have the game match you up with random gamers. (The game will find others ranked at a similar level as you.) Tap the "+" icon on the Home screen (located to the right and left of your chosen brawler) to invite one of your online friends at a time to join your team for an upcoming match.

*Make friends online by joining **Brawl Stars** Clubs or by inviting online friends to play with you. How to do this will be explained in Section 6— Join Some Online Clubs and Chat in this guide. For example, you can easily link your Facebook or LINE Connect account to your **Brawl Stars** account to find and interact with specific gamers.*

Each Brawler is Unique

Brawl Stars is much more than just a run-of-the-mill shooting/combat game. There are more than 27 unique brawler characters that can be unlocked (or purchased) and then controlled, but additional brawlers are constantly being introduced into the game.

Because each brawler has a unique appearance and fighting capabilities, you'll need to discover what sets your selected brawler apart and then learn how to tap those capabilities for offensive and defensive purposes during each match.

The better you get at controlling your favorite brawler, the bigger advantage you'll have. However, when playing with a partner or team, it's important to discover how to best utilize your own brawler's skills and capabilities while taking full advantage of what's special about the brawler(s) your partner or teammates are controlling.

Some combinations of brawlers work better together than others, since some are long-range fighters, as opposed to close-range fighters or healers. A lot also has to do with the arena you're in during a match, and what the objectives of the Event are that you're trying to accomplish.

When working with a partner or as part of a team, winning the match is obviously the most important task at hand. However, you're often rewarded for your own efforts and successes during each match. By performing well, you could earn the title Star Player, which comes with some added bonuses.

Each type of Event you participate in will have a unique objective (sometimes several objectives). You might need to collect a certain number of gems, gather the most stars, protect your team's safe, or defeat a pre-determined number of enemies in order to achieve victory.

*Keep in mind, because **Brawl Stars** is an online-based, real-time, multiplayer game, having a continuous and fast Internet connection is essential. If you see a red "poor Internet" icon appear on your screen, this will negatively impact your reaction time and hamper your brawler's capabilities during a match. If your Internet connection is too slow, you'll be ejected from the match altogether or could find yourself continuously getting defeated.*

To become an all-star gamer, you'll need to unlock, upgrade, and practice using each of the different brawlers, plus discover how to best utilize their unique capabilities during each type of match or challenge you encounter. You'll also need to become familiar with the terrain in each arena and use it to your advantage during matches.

Perfect timing and accurate aim are essential when engaging in combat (brawls), but if you want to be victorious when playing *Brawl Stars*, you'll need to learn when to rush enemies and attack versus when to hide, hang back from the action, or retreat away from the action so your brawler can replenish their Health and recharge their Attack capability. You'll also need to learn how and when to use each of your brawler's unique fighting capabilities, based on the challenges you're currently facing.

Knowing the strengths and weaknesses of each brawler will serve you well, but equally important is being able to outwit the gamers controlling each of the enemy brawlers. Each gamer will have their own gaming style and skill level that you'll need to quickly analyze and adapt to in order to outfight and outwit them during a match.

Especially when playing with and against random gamers, some will be newbs (beginners). You'll likely be able to predict the newb's actions and easily defeat the brawler they're controlling, especially when those brawlers still have a low Rank and Star Power level.

Other gamers, however, will have more experience and faster reflexes, and will know how to tap the full potential of the brawler they're controlling. These gamers will have also memorized each arena's layout and know how to navigate around it. These people will be your true adversaries, and likely the most difficult to outsmart and defeat.

From the moment each match begins, study your opponents and determine the best approach to take when you encounter them in the arena. You'll probably want to rush (attack) brawlers you identify as being controlled by newbs and attack them, and you might want to keep your distance (when possible) from brawlers who seem to be controlled by gamers with advanced skill and experience.

How close you should get to an enemy in the arena will depend on whether you've chosen to control a brawler who specializes in close-range or long-range combat, and what the capabilities are of the brawler you're currently facing.

Discover Your Main Objectives

Every type of Event featured within *Brawl Stars* has its own set of objectives. After choosing your brawler, tap the Event button (near the bottom center of the screen) to see a list of Events currently available or that can be instantly unlocked.

From this Choose Event screen, you'll see that Gem Grab is always available. Solo or Duos Showdown Events can be unlocked once you've collected 30 Trophies. As you can see here, Gem Grab and Showdown are the two Events that have been unlocked thus far. Once a gamer collects 150 total Trophies, the Daily Events slot will be unlocked. After collecting 350 total Trophies, Ticketed Events will become available. By collecting 800 total Trophies, the Special Events slot will also be unlocked (shown here on an iPad.)

Each Event takes place within an arena. Tap the circular Info ("i") icon seen in the top-right corner of each Event listing to see a detailed description of the Event along with a map of its arena.

Upon selecting the Showdown Event, choose between a Solo or Duo match. A Solo match requires your brawler to fight alone. A Duo match allows you to invite one partner to join you. This can be an online friend you choose, or a random gamer. The goal of a Showdown match is to eliminate all the other brawlers. Shown here is the Info screen for the Showdown Event that will take place within the Royal Runway arena.

During a Showdown match, collect green Power Cubes (one has been busted out of a chest and is shown near the center of the screen) to boost your brawler's Health and Attack damage capabilities. At the same time, be sure to avoid the clouds of toxic green smoke during the match.

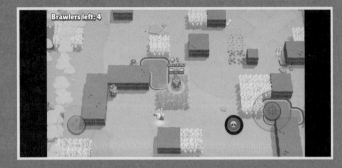

If you stumble upon an Energy Drink as you're traveling around within the arena during a match, be sure to grab it. This will give your brawler's Attack strength and speed a temporary boost. After consuming an Energy Drink, go on the offensive, rush your enemies, and launch attacks!

An Energy Drink is a bright-colored cup. They appear randomly in some arenas during a match.

Especially if you're a newb, checking out the Event Info screen before choosing an Event to participate in will help you understand the objectives during the upcoming match, plus allow you to study the arena's terrain before you're forced to engage in battle in that terrain.

When playing any 3 vs 3 brawler Event, such as Gem Grab, your team will benefit from assigning each brawler a role based on their unique capabilities. One brawler should be in charge of launching head-on, close-range attacks against enemies. The second brawler should be in charge of collecting and holding onto gems (while avoiding enemy attacks), and the third brawler should protect the brawler holding the gems but should be willing to defend the team's turf and help out whenever they're needed in battle.

Some expert **Brawl Stars** gamers believe it's better to choose your own team and assign each brawler a role (by communicating before a match), as opposed to allowing the game to randomly pick your teammates (and then you're not able to communicate with them). With practice, however, you can win matches and proceed through the game exclusively by playing with random gamers.

When you have the opportunity to choose your teammates from your online friends, select the best selection of brawlers to make up your team. A well-rounded team of brawlers will give you a tactical advantage. Since Supercell periodically tweaks each brawler's strengths and capabilities and updates the layout of the various arenas, the best brawlers to include within a team will change over time.

Keep in mind some brawlers perform better in certain arenas, and some are better at long-range combat as opposed to close-range combat. There are also Healers, who can help keep the Health of their teammates strong during matches.

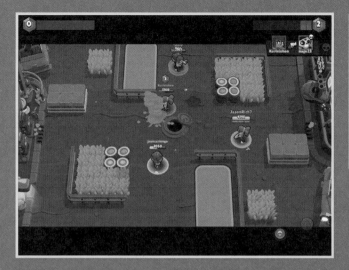

As a newb, don't worry too much about winning or losing matches. Instead, focus on getting comfortable navigating your brawler around the arena and engaging in battles. The longer you can stay alive during a match, the better.

One way to stay alive longer during a match is to keep pressing the on-screen Fire button in preparation for using your brawler's Super capability, as opposed to their normal Attack capability. When the Super capability is not available until it fully charges, the result will be that your brawler's Attack move is used. The moment the Super ability becomes available, however, it'll launch immediately and cause the mega-damage it's intended to.

During a match, displayed near the lower-left corner of the screen is the light blue Directional controller used to move your brawler around the arena. On the opposite side of the screen is the light red targeting tool. Place a finger on it and drag it in a specific direction to activate and then use the manual aiming tool for your brawler's Attack, Super, or Star Power capability. To the left of the red targeting tool is the Fire button. Tap this to launch your brawler's Attack, Super, or Star Power capability. Each time this icon turns yellow, the Super capability is fully charged. As it's recharging (which is done by achieving successful hits using your brawler's Attack capability), a recharge meter is displayed around the Fire button.

Keep in mind the Super move for some brawlers does not cause damage. It serves a different purpose during a match, so using it wisely will be more beneficial than randomly using it whenever it becomes available.

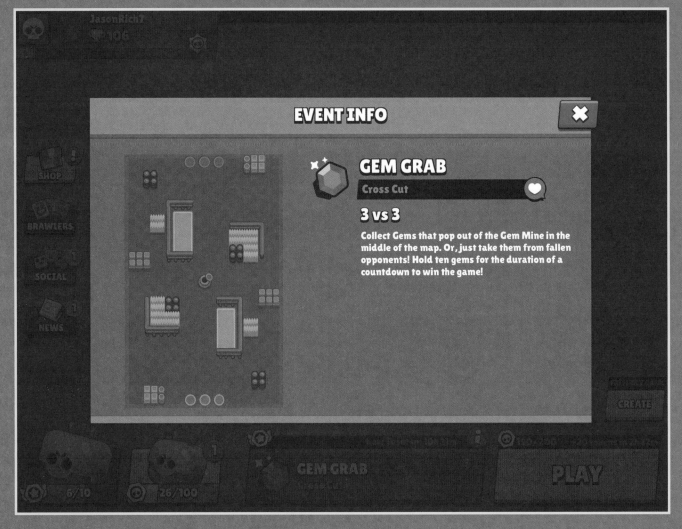

While you're still a newb, initially stick to playing one game play mode (Event type), such as Gem Grab, instead of switching between different Events that require different skills and strategies to master. Early on, you're better off spending more time brushing up your gaming skills for one Event at a time while you're also getting accustomed to working with a specific brawler. Bouncing between Events and constantly switching between brawlers requires you to master too many gaming skills at once in order to achieve success. Take your time and get good at one thing at a time, then move on to controlling new brawlers or participating in new types of Events, once you're able to achieve frequent victories.

Popular Types of Events

An Event in **Brawl Stars** is basically a game play mode. Some Events, like Gem Grab, are always available. Others need to be unlocked or are only available for a limited time. On an ongoing basis, different types of Events are introduced into the game.

Solo Showdown places you in an arena alone against 10 other brawlers. Your goal is to defeat everyone else and be the last brawler standing at the end of the match. If your brawler gets defeated and eliminated from the match, it's over for you. There's no respawning in this Event. When you win a match, you receive a bunch of Trophies. However, each time you lose a match, Trophies are often taken away, based on how you placed. If you place 1st, 2nd, 3rd, 4th, or 5th in a Solo Showdown Event, you'll win a certain number of Trophies. But if you place 6th, 7th, 8th, 9th, or 10th during this type of Event, a pre-determined number of Trophies will be taken away from you. (This also applies when playing a Duo Showdown match.)

If you're a newb, Solo Showdown offers the easiest way to increase your stash of Trophies and quickly progress through Trophy Road (at least initially), especially if you're consistently able to achieve fifth place or better during each match. However, other game play modes, such as Gem Grab, will allow you to upgrade your individual brawlers a bit faster. At the start of a Showdown match, if you simply hide in a bush and allow enemies to battle each other, you can remain safe until only five brawlers remain. At this point, you're guaranteed to win at least one Trophy or more (as opposed to losing Trophies), depending on how much longer you stay in that match.

Showdown Duo *allows you to team up with one other gamer—either at random or an online friend—and compete against five other teams of two. The gamer (or team) that's the last to remain alive at the end of the match wins. If your goal is to win as many Trophies as possible, it's essential that your team comes in first or second (out of five teams) during each match. Each player on the first-place team wins six Trophies. The players on the second place team win three Trophies. The third-place team neither gains nor loses Trophies. However, the fourth and fifth place team members lose Trophies.*

Gem Grab *is the most popular Event in the game. Gems periodically spawn in the center of the arena. This is a 3 vs 3 brawler gaming mode. One team is based at the top of the arena and the other at the bottom. The goal is for your team to collect 10 purple gems and hold onto them for 15 seconds to win the match. When a brawler gets defeated, based on which team they're from, they'll respawn at the top or bottom of the arena after about three seconds.*

Bounty *is an event that pits two teams of three gamers each against each other. The goal is to collect stars by defeating enemy brawlers. Every time a brawler defeats one enemy, their bounty of stars increases (up to a maximum of seven stars). Likewise, when a brawler gets defeated, their team loses stars, but the brawler will respawn and be able to continue fighting. When the two-minute timer runs out at the end of the match, the team holding the most stars wins.*

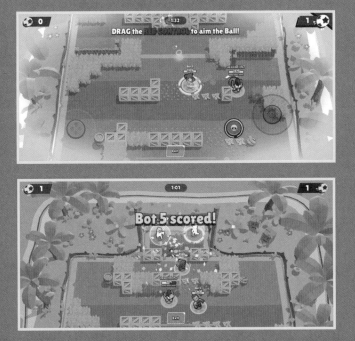

Heist is 3 vs 3 gaming mode that requires each brawler to help keep their team's safe protected, while at the same time try to break into and destroy the opposing team's safe. Each safe has an HP level. When it reaches zero, the safe gets destroyed and the match ends. One team's safe is located at the top of the arena, and the other team's safe is found at the bottom of the arena. The team that busts open the enemy team's safe first wins the match. However, if time runs out (after two and a half minutes), it's the team that caused the most damage to the opposite team's safe that wins the match.

Brawl Ball is also a 3 vs 3 gaming mode, but during the matches, the objective is to take control of a ball and get it into the opposing team's goal to score. The first team to score two goals wins the match. Of course, at the same time you'll be fighting enemy brawlers. If you're the one holding the ball, make your way to the opposing side's goal while trying to avoid enemies altogether. However, when it's one of your teammates carrying the ball, take it upon yourself to protect them and try to eliminate enemy brawlers that get too close to the teammate holding the ball.

One useful strategy when participating in a Heist match is to have two of the three teammates focus on distracting the opposing team while the third teammate utilizes a route along the side of the arena to get to the opposing side's safe to attack it from the side or from behind. Since most attacks tend to come from the center of the arena, utilizing a side path is often less expected and goes unguarded. The brawler attacking the safe should have a long-range weapon at their disposal so they can start shooting at the safe from a distance.

Siege requires gamers to participate on a three-brawler team. The goal is to find and destroy the opposing team's IKE Assembly Turret. At the same time, you and your teammates need to find Bolts and feed them to your team's Assembly Turret to construct a mighty Siege Robot who will serve as a soldier for your team. The more Bolts your team's Robot receives, the stronger it'll become. Each time a brawler is defeated, they'll respawn near the team's IKE Assembly Turret after about three seconds. The team that destroys the enemy's Turret or robot first wins. If the timer hits zero before the destruction happens, the team that caused the most damage on their enemy's Turret or Siege Robot is declared the winner.

As a gamer, once you collect 350 Trophies playing any combination of **Brawl Stars** Events, the ability to participate special Ticketed Events will be unlocked. Once this happens, you'll first need to purchase or win Tickets to enter these matches. Some Ticketed Events require you (and your teammates) to fight and defeat a powerful, game-controlled Boss robot and his army of henchmen bots. This is a difficult challenge that requires skill, experience, teamwork, and quick reflexes. If you achieve victory, however, the rewards are awesome!

One of the several different Ticketed Events is called ***Big Game***. *This one is a bit different from all others. A single team of five brawlers, each controlled by a separate gamer, must defeat one super-powered brawler being controlled by a sixth gamer.*

Big Brawler is the main opponent in a Big Game Event. He has more powerful attack capabilities than the other brawlers, plus his Health meter has an extra-large capacity so he can stay alive longer. The goal is to defeat Big Brawler as quickly as possible, or at least before the match timer counts down to zero.

Boss Fight *is the name of another Ticketed Event. This one requires a team of three brawlers to defeat a powerful Boss robot.*

Ticketed Events are only available on weekends, and since there are so many different types of matches, before paying your Ticket and entering the match, check the Info screen so you know exactly what your objectives are.

By studying the arena map for a Big Game Event, for example, you can quickly determine that because this particular arena is divided into so many boxes (using solid walls), brawlers with close-range combat capabilities will likely perform better. However, if you're using a brawler with long-range fighting techniques, targeting Big Boss from different angles while avoiding his forward-facing attacks will be essential. Rico's bouncing bullets will be particularly useful, for example, since they'll bounce around and travel in between the arena's many walled-in areas.

From the Choose Event screen, you'll see what Events are currently available. When you see one of the Event slots says New Event!, tap it. This will reveal a new Event you can participate in, plus award you with a collection of bonus Tokens. So to collect the free bonus Tokens, be sure to open any new Events that become available each day, even if you don't plan to experience them. Tokens need to be collected to unlock Brawl Boxes, which contain goodies.

In some cases, a newly unlocked Event will be similar to an Event you've previously unlocked, but a new arena map will be featured. The first time you win a newly unlocked Event each day, you'll receive one Star Token. These Star Tokens are used to unlock Big Boxes. It takes 10 Star Tokens to unlock each Big Box.

Collecting and Using Coins, Gems, Tokens, Power Points, and Star Points

As you experience all of the different types of Events within **Brawl Stars**, there are many different items to collect that'll help keep your brawler in a match, boost their level, and help you make your way along Trophy Road, for example.

Gold Coins are used to upgrade your brawler between matches. Bundles of these Coins can typically be found within Brawl Boxes, Big Boxes, or Mega Boxes (each of which are loaded with goodies once you're able to open them). Bundles of Coins can also be purchased from the Shop using Gems (which cost real money). Here, a bundle of 17 Coins was one of the rewards for opening a Brawl Box.

As you can see here, Tara is about to be upgraded to Power Level 2 at a cost of 20 Coins. The amount of her Health meter, along with her Attack and Super capabilities, will be increased as a result of the upgrade is listed on the right side of the screen.

Green Gems are used to buy Big Boxes, Mega Boxes, Skins, Coin Packs, Token Doublers, and other items sold within the Shop. Gems cost real money. Bundles of Gems can be purchased for between $1.99 (U.S.) and $99.99 (U.S.). As you can see, a Mega Box is about to be purchased for 60 Gems (around $5 US).

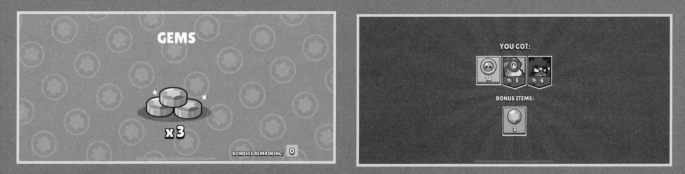

It is possible to randomly win a few Gems at a time by opening boxes, but it'll take a long time to win enough Gems to be able to actually acquire something useful from the Shop unless you also purchase additional Gem bundles using real money.

Be sure to check out the Shop on a daily basis. Each day you can claim a free item from below the Daily Deals heading or use Coins (as opposed to Gems) to purchase certain items, such as Power Points for specific brawlers. Power Points are used to upgrade specific brawlers. Shown here, the free item offered is two Tickets. Simply tap the Free slot to redeem the prize, then return to the Shop 24 hours later to redeem a different prize. How the Shop looks on the screen continues to evolve over time.

In between matches, periodically visit the Brawlers screen by tapping the Brawlers icon on the right side of the Home screen to upgrade individual brawlers, once upgrades have been earned. Shown here, two of the four brawlers (Shelly and Nita) can be upgraded. Once you earn enough Power Points to upgrade a brawler's Power Level, you must then purchase the upgrade using Coins. The higher the Power Level a brawler achieves, the more Power Points (and Coins) you'll need for their next upgrade. Each brawler can be upgraded up to Power Level 10.

After each match, if you've won the match or have proven yourself in other ways as a skilled brawler, you'll typically earn Trophies. Collecting Trophies allows you to travel your way along Trophy Road and be able to unlock new brawlers, boxes, Events, and other power-ups once you reach specific milestones.

As of summer 2019, to reach the end of Trophy Road and unlock all the prizes it had to offer you'd need to win 14,500 Trophies. Don't worry, even if you're a pro gamer, this task will keep you very busy for a long time. Plus, it's likely Trophy Road will expand in the future, allowing you to unlock even more prizes by collecting additional Trophies.

Each time you lose a match or don't achieve its objectives, however, one or more Trophies will be taken away from your stash, which will slow down your progress along Trophy Road.

Typically, winning battles during matches also allows you to earn Tokens, which are collected and used to open Brawl Boxes. It takes 100 Tokens to unlock and open a Brawl Box. Displayed above the Play button on the Home screen is a timer, along with the number of Tokens currently up for grabs. Once you've collected all of the available Tokens, you'll need to wait for the timer to reset to again win Tokens for achieving success during matches. Even without winning Tokens, you can brawl as much as you want and just focus on collecting Trophies.

Yet another form of in-game currency within **Brawl Stars** is called Star Points.

Star Points are collected during game play and are used to buy exclusive items from the Shop. The number of Star Points you currently have is always displayed near the top-center of the screen, along with counters that show how many Tickets, Coins, and Gems you currently possess.

After helping to win a match, Colt earned one Star Token, six Trophies, and 32 Tokens, but because a Token Doubler was active, he wound up with 64 Tokens.

While visiting the Shop, scroll to the right and look for the Star Shop heading. Below it, you'll see a selection of items that can be acquired by redeeming Star Points. Shown here, the Outlaw Colt skin can be purchased for 500 Star Points, and the Linebacker skin for Bull can be purchased for 2,500 Star Points. These two offers expire in 12 hours and 19 minutes and will be replaced by new offers daily.

Do You Have What It Takes to Earn the Star Player Title?

One of the best ways to enhance your personal brawling skills is to take part in Friendly Games. When you do this, not only can you choose specific gamers to be on your team and to compete against, but during these matches, all of the brawlers will be fully upgraded. You can also participate in any of the Events offered within the game, even if you have not yet unlocked them.

Unfortunately, there are no Trophies or Tokens to be won by participating in Friendly Games, but the extra practice will make winning actual matches easier.

To create and participate in a Friendly Game, from the game's Home screen, tap the Create button.

From the Friendly Game screen, tap the Invite button for each brawler slot to invite specific gamers to be on your team or to play against your team. Any slots you don't fill with your online friends will automatically be filled by random gamers.

Many newbs tend to focus on upgrading and maxing out the capabilities of one brawler before moving on to the next. However, you'll progress faster through the game if you focus on unlocking as many brawlers as possible, and then try to play and upgrade them evenly.

Especially early on, don't just favor one brawler. Try to keep them even in terms of their Power Level. Doing this will also help you learn the strengths and weaknesses of each brawler. Later, when you're controlling your favorite brawler, you'll know what to expect from the enemies you encounter because you've had experience working with the brawlers you've unlocked.

While working with each individual brawler, focus on perfect timing and positioning when using their Attack, Super, and Star Power capabilities. As you're figuring this out for each brawler, get comfortable with the time it takes to replenish their Health and reload their Attack so when they're vulnerable you can take on a more defensive fighting stance.

Based on the vulnerabilities of a specific brawler, you also need to know when to retreat, seek cover (behind a wall), or hide (in a bush) in order to avoid enemies who are stronger or have some type of tactical advantage.

This unofficial encyclopedia will teach you a wide range of brawling tactics, Event winning strategies, and proven ways to protect your brawler (and your team) during matches. You'll learn some awesome techniques for using the terrain to your advantage, plus discover the best places to position your brawler when it comes to accomplishing specific tasks during matches.

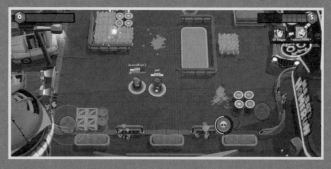

Knowing what to do and when to do it is only the first step. If you want to consistently win the Star Player title, you'll need to invest a lot of time actually playing **Brawl Stars**, *experience the different types of Events firsthand, and get comfortable working with the different brawlers. In other words, you'll need to practice a lot to become a really good player.*

Know When to Rush, Hide, Take Cover, or Retreat

During any match, there will be times when it's necessary for your brawler to rush an enemy in order to launch an attack. Rushing means you run directly toward the target as fast as possible, hopefully without attracting too much attention. Depending on the situation, you may or may not want to be using your Brawler's auto-aiming Attack move during your approach.

After shooting all three rounds of your brawler's Attack capability, it takes a few seconds for it to recharge, one ammo bar at a time. Notice the player named JasonRich7 has used up all three shots, so the ammo meter over his brawler's head is flashing red (meaning it's empty).

Meanwhile, any time you are *not* using your brawler's Attack, Super, or Star Power capability, their Health meter will slowly recharge. While the Attack capability or Health meter is recharging, consider taking cover behind a wall or any solid object for protection against many (but not all) types of incoming attacks. When you're behind a solid object such as a wall, enemies can still potentially see your brawler's position.

Any time your brawler stands still in the center of a bush, this allows them to hide and go unseen by enemies. During this time, their Health meter and Attack capability can recharge. However, if an enemy fires their Attack or Super capability into the bush or walks into the bush, the hiding brawler will get noticed. Especially when playing a Showdown Event, it makes sense to hide in a bush for the first few minutes so several of your enemies will eliminate each other while you don't do anything. Notice the green "+" over the Barley brawler being controlled by JasonRich7. He is currently hiding in the bushes on the left side of the arena, waiting for his Health and Attack capability to replenish.

As soon as you've launched all three rounds of your brawler's Attack capability, if the enemy target has not yet been defeated, you'll likely need to retreat (run in the opposite direction away from the enemy) to put as much distance between you and your adversary as possible.

Retreating becomes even more important if the enemy specializes in long-range combat. In some cases, if you have access to a long-range Attack capability, you might want to retreat while shooting, so you can inflict damage and maintain a safe distance from an enemy who possesses close-range fighting capabilities.

SECTION 2

HOW TO DOWNLOAD THE GAME AND GET STARTED

Brawl Stars is available for the Apple iPhone and iPad from the App Store, and from the Google Play Store for Android-based mobile devices. The first step is to download and install the game. Next, set up a free *Brawl Stars* account, and then get ready to rumble!

Is Playing *Brawl Stars* Really Free?

The good news is you can download and play *Brawl Stars* for free on an unlimited basis without seeing ads. However, without spending real money, it'll take you longer to unlock new brawlers, upgrade your brawlers, and acquire items that would otherwise be purchased from the Shop using green Gems.

Minimum Mobile Device Requirements

Before you can jump in and experience the nonstop brawling action in *Brawl Stars*, download and install the game onto your compatible mobile device. For starters, your mobile device will need at least 1GB of available RAM, although having more than 1.5G of RAM is recommended. Your mobile device will also need at least 1GB of available internal storage space, but 1.5GB of available storage space is recommended.

How to Download *Brawl Stars* on the iPhone or iPad

On an Apple iPhone or iPad, you must be running iOS 9.0 or later. To find and download it, follow these steps (shown here on an iPhone Xs Max):

- **Step #1**: From the Home screen, launch the App Store.

- **Step #2**: Tap the Search icon that's located at the bottom-right corner of the App Store screen.
- **Step #3**: In the Search field, type "*Brawl Stars*."
- **Step #4**: Either tap the Get button when you see the app listing for *Brawl Stars* or tap the game's title to access the App Store's Description screen.

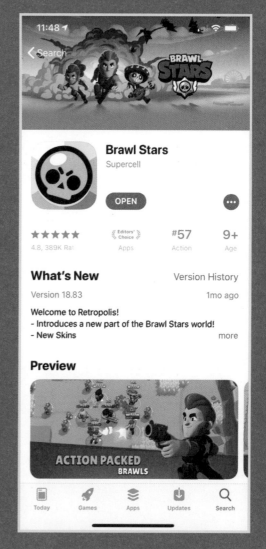

Step #5: Once the app is downloaded, tap the Open button while still in the App Store to launch the game, or from the Home screen, tap the newly created *Brawl Stars* app icon to launch the game.

Step #6: Tap the Okay button when the Important Notice window pops up on the screen.

- **Step #7**: When prompted, enter your name. All of your future teammates and other gamers you encounter online will see your name displayed.

You'll meet Shelly, the first Brawler you'll be able to control in the game. Follow the on-screen tutorial to learn some gaming basics. Whenever you play **Brawl Stars** *on a smartphone, you'll always hold it sideways, in landscape mode. (Shown here on an iPad.)*

- **Step #8**: Experience some additional practice brawls before you start competing for real.

Brawl Stars May Support a Controller When Running iOS 13

One of the features added to iOS 13 and iPad OS 13 is that it's possible to wirelessly link a PlayStation 4 or Xbox One controller to your smartphone or tablet in order to control a game's on-screen action using the gaming controller instead of the touchscreen controls. Whether or not **Brawl Stars** will be one of the compatible games you can use a controller with will be revealed in September 2019.

As of summer 2019, an Apple TV version of **Brawl Stars** had not yet been released. While it's possible to use the iPhone or iPad's "mirror" feature to display the game on your HD television set using an Apple TV device, the lag time will often negatively impact your gameplay experience.

How to Download and Install Brawl Stars on an Android-Based Mobile Device

Brawl Stars is a free game for Android mobile devices and available from the Google Play Store. Follow these steps to find, download, and install the game on to your Android-based smartphone or tablet (shown here on a Google Pixel 3a XL smartphone):

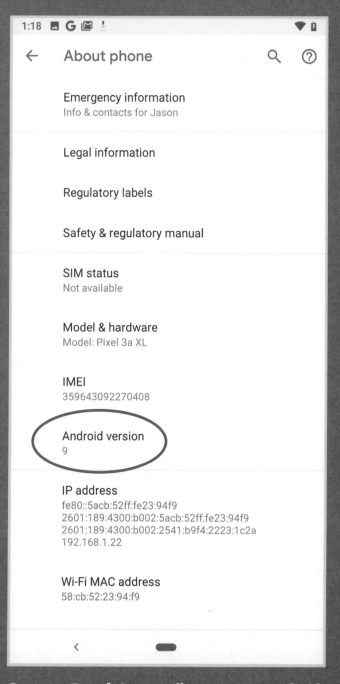

To see which version of the Android operating system your mobile device has installed, launch Settings and select the About Phone (Tablet) option. Depending on the device, you may need to tap on the General tab, select the About Device option, and then look for the Android Version subheading.

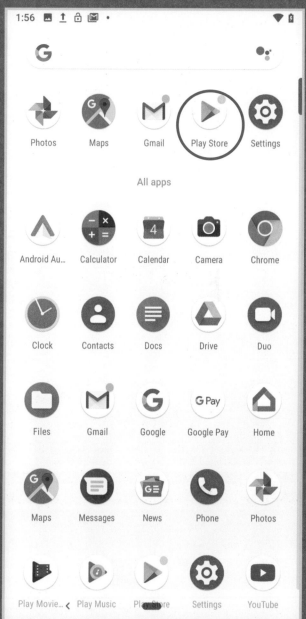

Step #1: *Brawl Stars will run on an Android-based mobile device running Android 4.3 or later, but it'll work best if your smartphone or tablet is running the Android 5 or later operating system. As you can see, this smartphone is running Android version 9.*

Step #2: *From the Home screen, launch the Google Play Store app.*

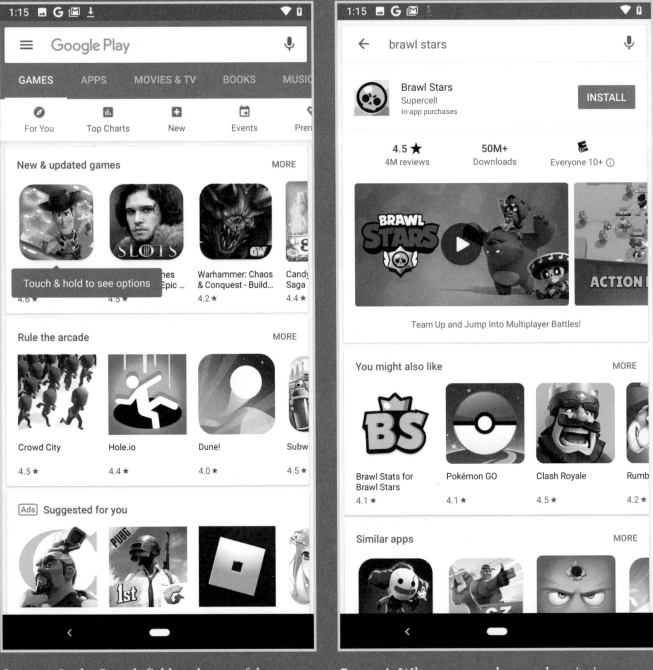

Step #3: *In the Search field at the top of the screen, type "**Brawl Stars**."*

Step #4: *When you see the app description screen for **Brawl Stars**, tap the Install button.*

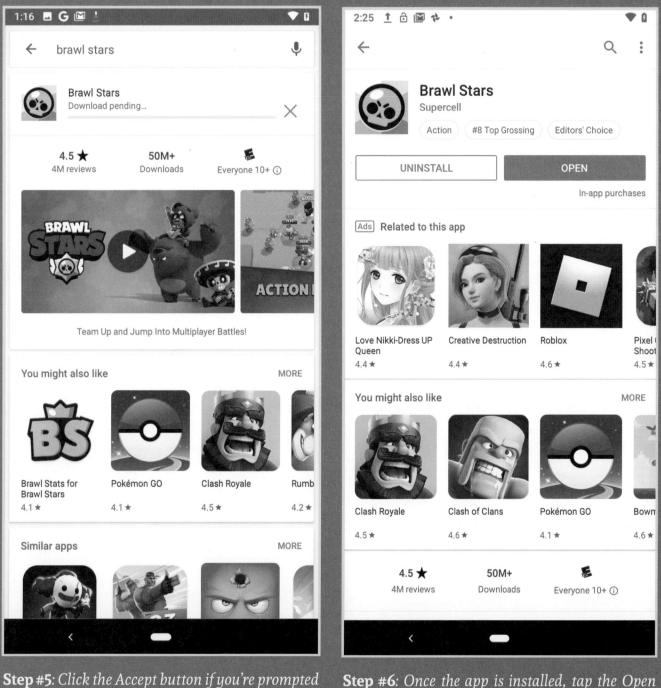

Step #5: *Click the Accept button if you're prompted to do so. It'll take a few minutes to download and install the game app onto your mobile device.*

Step #6: *Once the app is installed, tap the Open button to launch the game.*

Step #7: *You'll meet Shelly, the first Brawler you'll be able to control in the game. Follow the on-screen tutorial to learn some gaming basics. Keep in mind: whenever you play* **Brawl Stars** *on a smartphone, you'll always hold it sideways in landscape mode.*

Step #8: *When prompted, enter your name. All of your future teammates and the other gamers you encounter online will see your name displayed.*

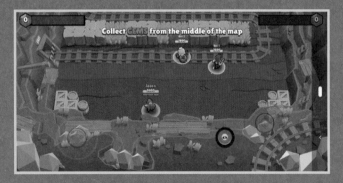

Step #9: *Experience some practice brawls before you start competing for real.*

Play *Brawl Stars* on a Windows PC or Mac

Currently **Brawl Stars** is only officially available for iOS and Android-based mobile devices. However, if you want to experience this mega-popular, ultra-fun, and incredibly challenging game on a Windows-based PC or Mac, this is possible using Bluestacks 4.

With more than 370 million users worldwide, Bluestacks 4 is an Android mobile emulator you can install onto your Windows PC or Mac for free, and then play your favorite Android-based games that are available from the Google Play store. The advantage to doing this is that you're able to control the on-screen action using your computer's mouse and keyboard (or a game controller), plus see all of the action unfold on your computer screen.

How to Install and Play *Brawl Stars* On a Windows PC or Mac

Step #1: *To play the Android version of* **Brawl Stars** *on your Windows PC or Mac using your favorite web browser on your computer, such as Microsoft Edge (PC), Google Chrome (PC or Mac), or Safari (Mac), visit www.bluestacks.com, and then click the Download Bluestacks button. This process could take 10 to 15 minutes, depending on the speed of your computer and Internet connection. It's shown here on a Windows PC.*

Step #2: *Once the Bluestacks software is installed, use Bluestacks to access the Google Play Store on your Internet-connected Windows PC or Mac. Sign in using your Google account.*

Step #3: *While visiting the Google Play Store, locate **Brawl Stars**, and then click the Install button near the top-right corner of the Bluestacks window to download and install it. Next, click the Open button to launch the game.*

Step #4: *The game will load just as it normally does on an Android-based smartphone or tablet.*

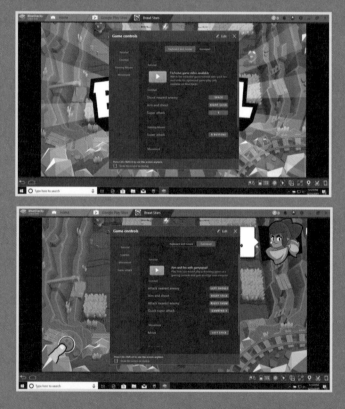

Step #5: *After installing **Brawl Stars**, use the default keyboard/mouse game controls that are displayed, or access this keymapping menu to customize the controls. When using Bluestacks on a PC or Mac, you can also play the game using an optional (and compatible) controller or gamepad.*

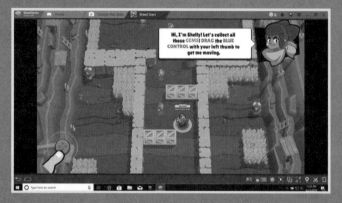

Step #6: *Play **Brawl Stars** just as you would on a mobile device, except you'll use your keyboard and mouse (or a controller/gamepad), as opposed to a touchscreen, to control the action. Shown here, **Brawl Stars** is running flawlessly on a Windows PC.*

Adjusting the *Brawl Stars* Game Settings

One of the first things you'll want to do after completing the **Brawl Stars** tutorial is access the game's main menu to adjust the various options offered by the Settings menu. (This process is shown here on an iPad.)

To access the Settings menu, tap the menu icon displayed in the top-right corner of the Home screen. It's shown here on an iPad and looks like three horizontal lines.

Tap the Settings menu option. It's on the right side of the screen.

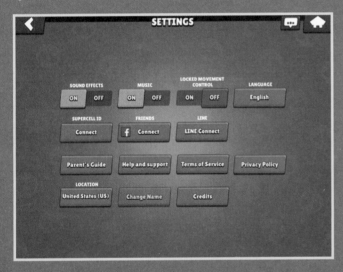

From the Settings menu, you're able to turn on/ off the Sound Effects and Music. While the sound effects play an important role in the game, the music is more for entertainment purposes, so you may want to turn off the music to eliminate the distraction.

Leave the Locked Movement Control virtual switch at the default Off position. When you turn on this feature, the on-screen controls for moving and shooting will remain in a specific position on the screen.

How to use the Supercell ID feature, how to link your gaming account to Facebook, and how to use the LINE Connect feature are covered later in this guide. What's more important right now is adjusting the Location option, if necessary.

Make sure the country option listed in the Location button is set to your home country. If not, tap this button, and from the Select Location menu screen, scroll down as needed and tap your home country. The supported countries are listed in alphabetical order.

When prompted, confirm your Location by tapping the Okay button. Your newly selected Location will now be listed in the Location button when viewing the Settings menu.

If you select a Location that's not your home country, your Internet connection could be slowed down—sometimes a lot. It's important to maintain the highest possible Internet connection speed when playing **Brawl Stars**. This is often achieved by connecting your mobile device to a Wi-Fi hotspot.

In some cases, you may discover a 4G LTE or 5G E cellular data Internet connection works best. Only use this option, however, if you have an unlimited cellular data plan, or you'll quickly use up your monthly cellular data allocation. When you're done adjusting the options listed in the Settings menu, tap the Home icon (located in the top-right corner of the screen). You're now ready to start brawling!

*Remember, anytime you attempt to play **Brawl Stars** using a slow Internet connection, you'll see a red "Poor Internet Connection" icon appear near the center of the screen. In some cases, you can keep playing. However, if the connection is too slow, the game will reset and return you to the Home screen.*

From the Settings menu, you're also allowed to change your name. This is the name other gamers see when you team up with them or oppose them before and during a brawl. You can't use the Change Name feature until you've reached Level 5. Until then, you'll need to use the name you initially entered when you first started playing.

Take Advantage of Supercell ID to Protect Your Account

As you progress through the game, unlock and upgrade your brawlers, and make in-app purchases to acquire items, all this information gets stored within your online-based **Brawl Stars** account.

It's important to protect your **Brawl Stars** account! While you can give out your username in order to connect with online friends within the game, never reveal your account password.

By turning on the optional Supercell ID feature built into the game, you can easily switch between gaming devices and play **Brawl Stars**, plus help to protect your gaming account from being hacked or stolen. Be sure to turn on the Supercell ID feature by following these steps:

Step #1: *From the Home screen, tap the Menu icon displayed in the top-right corner of the screen.*

Step #2: *Tap the Settings button displayed at the top of the menu.*

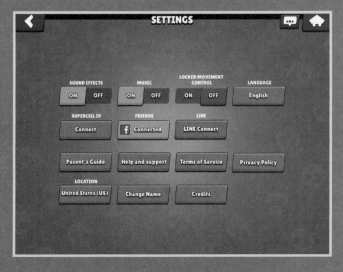

Step #3: *Tap the Connect button displayed below the Supercell ID heading in the Settings menu.*

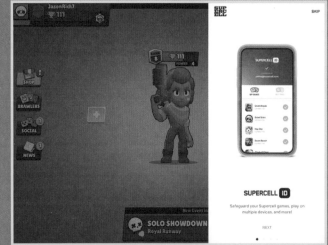

Step #4: *Scroll through the information screens that explain the Supercell ID feature or tap the Skip option (found in the top-right corner of the screen). Tap the Get Started option to continue.*

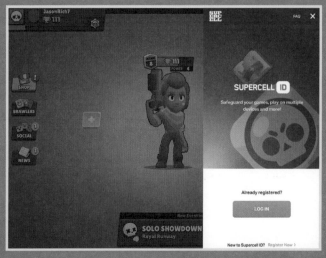

Step #5: *If this is your first time playing a Supercell game, select the Register Now option. You'll find this option near the bottom-right corner of the screen.*

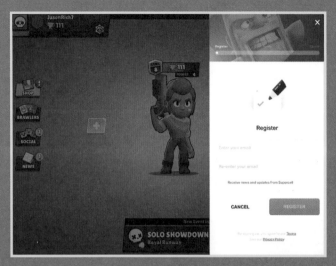

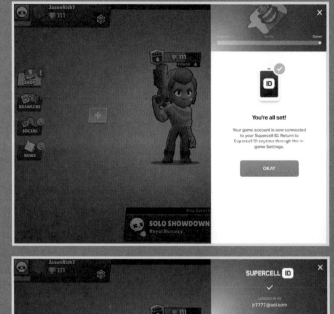

Step #6: *When prompted, enter your email address twice, and then tap the Register button.*

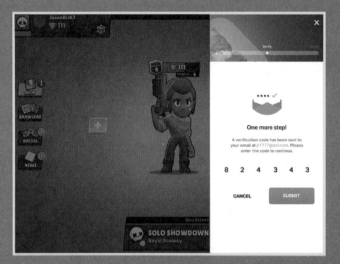

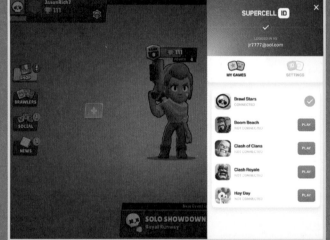

Step #7: *A six-character verification code will be emailed to you. (The number will be different from the one shown here.) When you receive the code, enter it into the verification screen, and then tap the Submit button.*

Step #8: *When the You're All Set! message appears on the screen, tap the Okay button. Your game account has now been connected to your Supercell ID. Exit out of the Supercell ID screen by tapping on the "X" icon. You're now ready to play* **Brawl Stars***.*

SECTION 3
MEET THE BRAWLERS

As of early summer 2019, *Brawl Stars* featured 27 unique brawlers. Each brawler is classified as being Common, Rare, Super Rare, Epic, Mythic, or Legendary, but can also be categorized based on their overall strengths as a fighter. Some brawlers are best suited for close-range combat. Others are more skilled at mid-range combat and/or offer some type of throwable (explosive) weapon. There are also brawlers who excel at long-range combat or at healing their teammates.

Prior to the start of each match, you're able to choose one brawler to control. If you're planning to be randomly paired up with other gamers, select the brawler you're most comfortable and experienced controlling. However, if you're manually selecting your partner or team, it's important for each person to choose a brawler with skills that complement each other.

Discover Each Brawler's Unique Skills and Capabilities

Beyond its rarity classification, each brawler has a main Attack, Super, and at least one (often more) Star Power capability, as well as a Health meter. Each time a brawler gets injured, some of their Health meter gets depleted. As soon as their Health meter is empty, that brawler gets removed from the match—either temporarily or permanently.

Depending on the Event type you're experiencing, a brawler may be able to automatically respawn at a specific spot within the arena about three seconds after they've been eliminated. This is the case when playing a Gem Grab match, for example. However, when playing other types of Events, like Showdown,

once your brawler is eliminated from the match, they're done for good. (You can always participate in another match, however.)

Health

Displayed above a brawler's head during each match is their Health meter, a solid green line when it's at 100 percent. Each time a brawler gets injured, some of their Health gets depleted.

There are, however, several ways to replenish or boost a brawler's Health during a match. Some brawlers serve as Healers and can boost the Health of their teammates while battles are taking place.

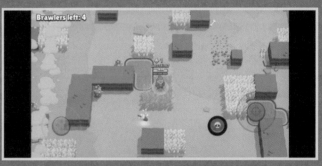

During some matches, a brawler can find and consume an Energy Drink to replenish some of their Health. There's a cup-shaped Energy Drink shown near the center of this screen (below the brawler being controlled by JasonRich7). Once it's consumed, your brawler will sparkle while the effects of the power-up are active. This includes replenished Health and the ability to temporarily move faster.

Hiding for a few seconds in a bush that's found in an arena also allows a brawler's Health meter to replenish faster, although it will slowly replenish on its own any time your brawler is participating in a match but not getting hit by incoming attacks or actively using their Attack or Super capabilities. Notice the Colt brawler being controlled by JasonRich7 has a green "+" icon near him. This indicates Colt's Health and Attack capability are being replenished.

Each time you upgrade a brawler's Power Level, the capacity of their Health meter increases, so they'll be able to stay alive longer and receive more damage before getting eliminated from a match.

The way to boost a brawler's Power Level is to collect Power Points. These are pink icons containing a lightning bolt. When a pre-determined number of Power Points have been collected, upgrading to the next Power Level requires you to redeem those Power Points, plus pay a pre-determined number of Coins.

In this case, Shelly has 30 out of the 30 Power Points needed to upgrade to Power Level 2. To proceed with this upgrade, the cost will be 35 Coins.

Power Points can typically be acquired from Brawl Boxes, Big Boxes, or Mega Boxes, or purchased in bundles from the Shop (typically using Coins). Brawl Boxes can be acquired by collecting and redeeming 100 Tokens. Big Boxes, which also often contain Power Point bundles, can be acquired by collecting and redeeming 10 Star Tokens, or by purchasing these boxes from the Shop for 30 Gems each. Mega Boxes can be purchased from the Shop for 80 Gems. These too contain a random selection of Power Point bundles for specific brawlers.

Continuously working to boost a brawler's Power Level increases their Health meter's capacity, so they're able to stay alive longer during matches because they can withstand more damage. A Health meter's capacity determines how many Hit Points (HP) a brawler can lose before their Health meter hits zero. Boosting a brawler's Power Level also improves the power of their Attack and Super capabilities, which determine how much damage they'll be able to inflict on their enemies during brawls.

Attack

Each brawler has a different Attack capability that's used to inflict damage on their enemies. Each time an Attack meter is fully charged, this gives you three shots before the Attack move needs to recharge. You can use all three shots in quick succession by pressing the Fire button three times quickly. However, it sometimes makes more sense to tap the Fire button just once, and wait until your target is properly lined up before taking additional shots.

If your brawler's Attack meter is empty, you'll need to wait a few seconds for it to recharge so at least one of the three segments is full before the Attack move can be used again. During this time, your brawler is vulnerable to incoming attacks. Consider hiding, retreating, or avoiding confrontations with enemies.

Depending on the Power Level of your brawler, how much damage their Attack capability causes with each shot will vary, as will the amount of time it takes to recharge. The higher a brawler's Power Level, however, the more damage each shot will cause.

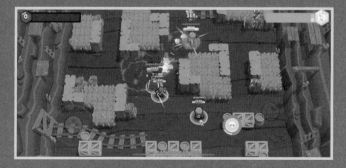

If you simply tap the Fire button, the Attack capability for the brawler you're using will automatically aim at the closest target. Check out the Loaded

Rico brawler being controlled by JasonRich7. The auto-aiming feature is being used to shoot the enemy brawler near the top-center of the screen.

When you use the manual Aiming feature, you can precisely aim each shot, but this process takes a bit longer. Shown here, Rico's Attack capability is being manually aimed at a specific enemy.

Super

Each brawler also has their unique Super capability. Depending on the brawler, this might be a close-range, mid-range, projectile, or long-range weapon, or a close-range fighting move. It could also be a healing tool or a way to temporarily travel around the arena much faster.

The amount of time it takes for a Super ability to recharge varies, but the more direct hits you inflict on an enemy (and the better your aiming accuracy) using your brawler's Attack move, the faster the Super capability will recharge. As for its ability to inflict damage, the higher your brawler's Power Level, the more damage their Super can cause.

Whenever possible, wait for your brawler's Super capability to fully charge, and then position your brawler in the right spot in the arena to use this capability in a way that will damage or heal multiple brawlers at once, depending on what the Super is designed to do. Perfect positioning and timing are essential for getting the most out of your brawler's Super ability.

Star Power

Once each brawler is upgraded to Power Level 9, their unique Star Power fighting capabilities can be unlocked. For example, one of Shelly's Star Powers is called Shell Shock. It unlocks and becomes available from a Brawl Box, Big Box, or Mega Box once she reaches Power Level 9. Nita's Star Power is called Bear With Me. It also unlocks and becomes available when this brawler reaches Power Level 9.

In addition to the Star Power listed for each brawler within this guide, Supercell has announced that throughout summer 2019, new Star Powers are being incorporated into the game, so be on the lookout for these new capabilities that'll improve the brawling skills of your favorite brawlers! You'll discover many of the brawlers can now unlock at least two distinct Star Powers. Once more than one Star Power becomes available to your brawler, you'll need to select just one that you want access to during each upcoming match.

You'll learn more about each of the 27 brawlers' unique Attack, Super, and Star Power capabilities later in this section.

The amount of damage per second (DPS) each Attack, Super, and Star Power move is capable of generating varies based on several factors, including which brawler you're controlling, the accuracy of your aim, and the current Power Level of the brawler. The higher their Power Level, the more DPS you'll inflict with each well-aimed attack. When looking at a brawler's profile screen, tap the Info ("i") icon associated with their Attack or Super capability to see how much DPS it can cause, based on that brawler's current Star Power level (which in this case is four).

How to Upgrade Your Brawlers

To recap, boosting a brawler's Power Level expands the capacity of their Health meter while boosting the strength of that brawler's Attack and Super capabilities. Upgrading a brawler's Power Level is done by collecting and redeeming Power Points. Once you've acquired the pre-requisite number of Power Points to level up, upgrading costs a pre-determined number of Coins.

In between matches, if you've earned enough Power Points and have the required number of Coins to upgrade a brawler's Power Level, do it as soon as possible. However, if you want to experience what a brawler is like when all of their capabilities have been maxed to their highest levels, participate in a Friendly Game using that brawler.

It takes less time to upgrade a brawler when you acquire Power Point bundles (brawler-specific bundles that can be purchased using Coins or in some cases Gems) from the Shop, or when you purchase (or acquire) Big Boxes, Brawl Boxes, or Mega Boxes. The Shop is shown here. On this day, from below the Daily Deals heading, four different Power Point bundles were available, each for a different brawler.

Upon purchasing and opening a Mega Box, among the prizes received were four Power Point bundles, each for a different brawler.

Get to Know the Brawlers

Take the time needed to familiarize yourself with each of the different brawlers. The first one you'll unlock when you begin playing **Brawl Stars** is Shelly. In this section, the brawlers are listed by name in alphabetical order.

After participating in a few successful matches with Shelly, as you progress along Trophy Road, you'll be able to unlock Nita (once you acquire 10 Trophies), Colt (once you acquire 60 Trophies), Bull (once you acquire 250 Trophies), Jessie (once you acquire 500 Trophies), Brock (once you acquire 1,000 Trophies), Dynamike (once you acquire 2,000 Trophies), Bo (once you acquire 3,000 Trophies), and Tick (once you acquire 4,000 Trophies). Trophy Road is shown here, and Bull is about to be unlocked after collecting more than 250 Trophies.

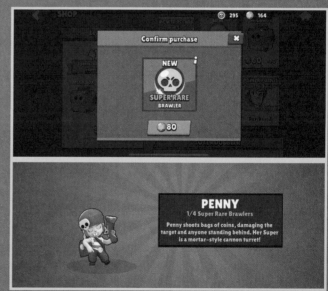

Beyond the brawlers that can be unlocked from Trophy Road by collecting Trophies, others can be randomly unlocked by acquiring and opening Brawl Boxes, Big Boxes, and/or Mega Boxes, or by purchasing and unlocking a mystery brawler offer from the Shop. Shown here, a Super Rare mystery brawler who turned out to be Penny was purchased as a Daily Deal from the Shop for 80 Gems (approximately $4.99 US).

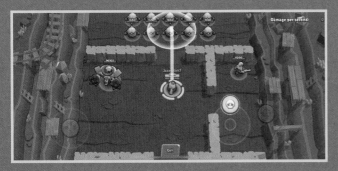

To test a brawler before you unlock them, from the Brawlers screen select one brawler that's still locked. From that Brawler's profile screen, tap the Try button.

You'll be transported to the Training Cave, where you can control the selected brawler. You don't receive any Trophies or rewards for time spent in the Training Cave, but you do have the chance to fine-tune your fighting skills using the brawler you select. Shown here, Spike's Super capability (called Stick Around!) is being manually aimed at the enemy bots located near the top-center of the screen.

Barley

Description	This robotic brawler carries a bottle of toxic liquid that he's all too happy to toss at enemies to neutralize them. When multiple bottles get tossed at or around opponents, Barley is able to cause even more damage and destruction.
Rarity Classification	Rare
Brawler Type	Thrower

Barley has just been unlocked. A random Rare brawler was offered as a Daily Deal from the Shop. It cost 30 Gems to unlock him.

At Power Level 5, for example, Barley's Health meter maxes out at 2880HP. His Attack capability increases to 816HP damage per second, and his Super capability increases to 816HP per second. Ten more Power Points are required before Barley can be upgraded to Power Level 6. Once the required points are collected, it'll cost 290 Coins to unlock the upgrade.

	Name	Description
Attack Capability	Undiluted	Each time Barley tosses one of his bottles and it smashes on the ground, any enemies caught in the splash zone of the poison liquid immediately receive damage. The longer an enemy stays in the leftover puddle, the more damage they'll receive.
Super Capability	Last Call	Instead of just throwing just one bottle filled with toxic sludge at his enemies, when Last Call is used, multiple bottles get thrown at the same time. More damage is caused as a result of the initial splash, plus the size (diameter) of the toxic liquid pool winds up being much larger, so it covers a wider area. This means it can cause even more damage, potentially to multiple enemies that get caught in the puddle.
Star Power Capability	Medical Use	Once activated (upon reaching Power Level 9), each time Barley launches an Attack, his Health meter also regains 300HP (until it gets maxed out).

Barley has several optional skins available. Shown here is Golden Barley (price: 30 Gems), which allows him to dress in a more formal looking suit.

This is what Wizard Barley looks like. As you can see, this outfit makes him look like a magical wizard. You'll receive this skin for free when you use the Connect Supercell ID feature in conjunction with your **Brawl Stars** account.

Bakesale Barley (price: 30 gems) dresses this robot in a blond wig and a bright pink dress. His bottle of toxic liquid is replaced by a poison pie.

Maple Barley causes this robotic brawler to look like someone who makes maple syrup. Thus, he carries what appears to be a maple syrup bottle, although its contents are toxic. This skin can be purchased from the Shop. Initially, skins were purchased using Gems. However, with the introduction of Star Points, this is also now an in-game currency used to acquire some skins.

Consider using Barley's Last Call (his Super capability) to attack the location you anticipate your enemies are heading to, as opposed to attacking the enemies directly where they're currently standing. Try to create blockades on the ground using the toxic liquid and force your adversaries to walk through the poison sludge so they receive damage.

Bibi

Description	Armed with a powerful bat and a mouth full of bubble gum, Bibi is a brawler to be reckoned with, especially when she engages in close-range combat.
Rarity Classification	Epic
Brawler Type	Batter (Close-Range Fighter)

Bibi is primarily a close-range brawler, so to survive in arenas during matches, she'll need to outmaneuver long-range projectile weapon attacks launched at her. By hiding and then jumping out at enemies who get close, she'll have a bigger advantage when she battles them. The key to launching a successful Attack is to first get close to the enemy, hopefully without being detected during her approach.

	Name	Description
Attack Capability	Three Strikes	Her main weapon is a baseball bat. When the bat is fully charged, Bibi has three swings that allow her to hit a Home Run and deal a blow to any enemies who are close by. In addition to inflicting damage on those she hits, her unfortunate targets will get knocked backwards.
Super Capability	Spitball	Bibi uses bubble gum from her mouth as a bouncing ball that she hits with her bat. The flying bubble gum ball will smash through enemies, bounce around, and has the ability to hit the same target multiple times (inflicting added damage with each direct hit).
Star Power Capability	Home Run	Once activated upon reaching Power Level 9, each time Bibi hits a Home Run (which occurs when her bat is fully charged), her movement speed will temporarily increase. This allows her to chase after enemies as she's attacking, or quickly retreat after launching an attack.

Whichever brawler you're controlling during a match, keep an eye on their Health meter and know when you need to retreat from a fight to seek refuge. Try to enter into brawls with your brawler's Health meter and Attack capability fully charged. The more direct hits you make with your brawler's Attack capability, the faster their Super capability recharges. As soon as you see it's available, determine the best place in the arena to be standing (based on the position of your enemies) to use that Super ability effectively. Bibi is being controlled here by JasonRich7. She's on the left side of the arena, replenishing her Health and Attack while hiding in a bush.

Bo

Description	Bo is big and muscular. He's also fierce looking while wearing his eagle hat. You'll discover he's a highly skilled archer.
Rarity Classification	Unlock this brawler from Trophy Road by collecting 3,000 Trophies.
Brawler Type	Fighter: Bo is best at long-range fighting. When you aim his bow, you can see how far his exploding arrows will fly (and still maintain their aiming accuracy).

Bo fights best when he can stay clear of close-range brawlers and concentrate on aiming his arrows at enemies from a distance. When enemies are on the move, you'll need to anticipate what direction they're headed, what sudden turns they might make, and then aim so the enemies walk into the approaching arrows that Bo shoots.

	Name	Description
Attack Capability	Eagle-Eyed	Each time his bow and arrows are used, three exploding arrows are released in the direction they're aimed. Each arrow can cause damage to its target. By shooting three shots in a row, that's a total of nine damage-causing arrows that can be launched quickly before the Attack needs to recharge.
Super Capability	Catch a Fox	Bo is able to plant hidden traps in the arena. When an enemy steps on a trap, it explodes, knocks the enemies backwards, and inflicts damage. This weapon takes a few seconds to set up, but it has the potential to dole out some mega-damage.
Star Power Capability	Circling Eagle	Once Bo reaches Power Level 9 and unlocks this capability, he can spot enemies hiding in bushes from twice the distance they can otherwise be spotted from.

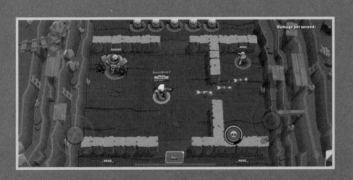

When using Bo's Eagle-Eyed attack, the arrows will spread out while in midair, so they could potentially hit multiple targets at once. But each individual arrow will inflict less damage than if the three arrows were to strike the same target at once.

Brock

Description	Armed with a blaster, this urban warrior shows no fear when entering into battle. His weapon shoots a barrage of long-range explosive missiles that inflict damage on all enemies he strikes. This weapon can also be used to destroy walls and other solid objects found in the arena that enemies could otherwise use for cover.
Rarity Classification	Unlock this brawler from Trophy Road by collecting 1,000 Trophies.
Brawler Type	Sharpshooter

Like any brawler who specializes in long-range combat, Brock will be at a disadvantage if he allows enemies with close-range fighting capabilities to get too close. If he can't shoot them from a distance, he's better off running away to put some distance between himself and his adversaries before using his Attack capability on them.

	Name	Description
Attack Capability	Rockin' Rocket	Each time Brock pulls the trigger on his rocket launcher, an exploding rocket is launched. It travels quickly to its target. This weapon works best from a distance.
Super Capability	Rocket Rain	When fully charged, Brock can shoot multiple rockets at once toward his target to inflict an even greater level of damage on his enemies or destroy a solid object (such as a wall) in the arena. As with any Super capability, you'll achieve better accuracy when you manually aim Rocket Rain as opposed to using the game's auto-aiming feature.
Star Power Capability	Incendiary	Once this capability is unlocked upon reaching Power Level 9, each time Brock launches a Rocket, it sets the ground on fire around its point of impact. For every second an enemy gets caught in the flame, they receive an extra 300HP worth of damage to their Health meter.

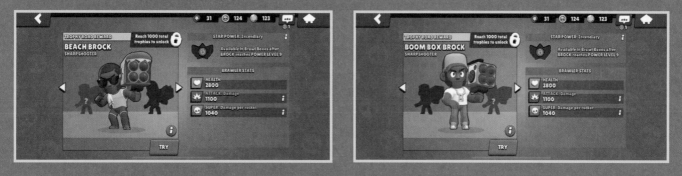

Like all the brawlers, Brock has an assortment of optional skins that can be purchased or unlocked. With his Beach Brock outfit, this urban fighter trades in his jeans, T-shirt, vest, and sunglasses for more casual beach attire. When he wears his Boom Box Brock outfit, his rocket launcher becomes a boom box.

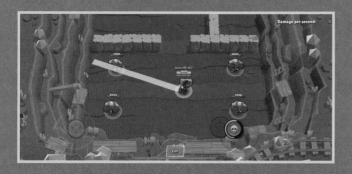

Brock's Rockin' Rocket can be manually aimed (shown here), or you can take advantage of the auto-aim feature and the Attack will automatically be targeted toward the closest enemy (or object).

Bull

Description	Big hair and bigger muscles make this brawler a fearsome foe in battle. However, when close to his enemies, his shotgun's bullets are what will cause some serious damage.
Rarity Classification	Unlock this brawler from Trophy Road by collecting 250 Trophies.
Brawler Type	Heavyweight

This is what Brock's Rocket Rain Super capability looks like when it's being shot at an enemy bot in the Training Cave.

Most brawlers who are armed with a projectile weapon such as a pistol or shotgun fight better from a distance when using their Attack capability. This is not the case with Bull. His shotgun causes more damage when it's shot from close range, so plan your attacks accordingly when controlling this brute.

	Name	Description
Attack Capability	Double-Barrel	To take full advantage of Bull's double-barrel shotgun, you'll need to move in really close to your enemies. Each time you pull the trigger, bullets will fly.
Super Capability	Bulldozer	Forget guns and bullets; when Bull gets angry, he'll lower his head and charge at enemies like a fierce and fearless bull. The Bulldozer move will inflict damage on enemies and allow Bull to smash through objects, such as solid walls, in the arena.
Star Power Capability	Berserker	After activating this capability by reaching Power Level 9, anytime Bull's Health meter drops below 40 percent capacity, the meter's recharge speed doubles.

Bull has a handful of optional skins, including Touchdown Bull, where he dresses up like a football quarterback for his brawls. To unlock this skin, it'll cost you 80 Gems (about $4.99 US).

Viking Bull (price: 80 Gems) allows Bull to disguise himself as a blond Viking. (Remember, some skins are now purchased using Star Points, which can be earned, instead of using Gems, which typically need to be acquired using real money.)

Bull works best at really close range when it comes to launching attacks, so be creative when you sneak up on enemies you know have long-range weapons. Perhaps you can have Bull hide in a bush (where he's virtually invisible), and then start attacking when an enemy approaches. Don't rely on having Bull take damage to his Health meter while absorbing incoming attacks as he approaches enemies. This won't always work. The right combination of incoming attacks launched by an enemy could drain Bull's Health meter before he's close enough to launch his own close-range attack.

Shown here, Bull's Double-Barrel attack is being shot at an enemy near the center of the screen. Notice the group of blue pellets flying through the air. This weapon has a spread associated with it, so the farther the bullet pellets need to travel, the wider the spread becomes.

Bull's Bulldozer Super capability has a much far-ther range. Shown here, the manual aim feature is being used to target specifically where this attack will land.

Carl

Description	Carl is a coal-mining robot armed with a Pickaxe that works like a boomerang. He rides in a small mining cart to get around the arena while he whacks away at whomever gets in his way.
Rarity Classification	Super Rare
Brawler Type	Fighter

The trick to controlling Carl is to understand how he maneuvers with his wheeled mining cart. Practice moving around, making sharp turns and pivoting to launch attacks, and rushing enemies when it's time to launch an attack. The Training Cave is a good place to practice maneu-vering around an arena and working with Carl's weapons.

	Name	Description
Attack Capability	Pickaxe	Carl tosses his Pickaxe at enemies. After it travels through the air and hopefully hits its target, it returns to Carl's hands so he can give it another throw. As you'd expect, each time the Pickaxe hits an enemy, it causes some damage. This is more of a long-range attack move.
Super Capability	Tailspin	This is a close-range attack that causes Carl to spin around in his mining cart for a few seconds and inflict harm on whomever he hits. Carl is one of the few brawlers able to fight at close-range or long-range with equal finesse.
Star Power Capability #1	Power Throw	Upon reaching Power Level 9, Carl can automatically throw his Pickaxe in a way that makes it travel faster, and then return to him so he can throw it again sooner. In other words, he can cause more damage in less time on the enemies he targets.
Star Power Capability #2	Protective Pirouette	This second Star Power also kicks in once Power Level 9 has been reached and it's been unlocked. While Carl is using Tailspin, he'll receive 30 percent less damage from incoming attacks.

One of the available skins for Carl is called Road Rage Carl. It transforms his mining cart into a clutch mini-racing car and his Pickaxe into a throwable wrench. This skin can be unlocked for 80 gems (about $4.99 US).

Carl's Pickaxe has been tossed. It was aimed at an enemy located near the bottom-right corner of the screen. After hitting its target (which in this case was another Carl brawler being controlled by an opposing gamer), the Pickaxe automatically returns to the thrower.

As you're controlling any brawler, when you have the time, manually aim their Attack at an enemy. In this case, the white line shows in which direction the Pickaxe Attack is being aimed, as well as

its range. Once tossed, the Pickaxe will reach the bottom-center of the screen. There is an enemy being targeted. He's hiding behind a wall, but by manually aiming the Attack, a direct hit is almost guaranteed (unless the target quickly moves).

Colt

Description	Colt thinks of himself as a debonair cowboy and is armed with a pair of shotguns. His main skill is being a sharpshooter, so he's at his best when attacking his targets from a distance.
Rarity Classification	Unlock this brawler from Trophy Road by collecting 60 Trophies.
Brawler Type	Sharpshooter

When using Colt's Six-Shooter Attack, it's only possible to shoot in a straight line. The ammo won't bounce off of solid objects, so it's important to line up your shots and not waste ammo. You only get three shots before a Six-Shooter needs to recharge.

	Name	Description
Attack Capability	Six-Shooter	Each time Colt uses this Attack, he simultaneously shoots six rounds of bullets from the two pistols he's carrying. If he's moving while shooting, the spread of the bullets will cover a larger area. If he stands still and aims, all six shots get focused on one primary target.
Super Capability	Bullet Storm	When Bullet Storm is used, Colt is able to rain bullets on his rivals to cause even more damage. This attack can also be used to destroy or smash solid items in the arena, such as walls or barriers his enemies are hiding behind.
Star Power Capability #1	Slick Boots	As soon as Colt reaches Power Level 9 and unlocks this ability, he's able to move around the arena faster because he's given a flashy new pair of boots.
Star Power Capability #2	Magnum Special	This second Star Power also kicks in once Power Level 9 has been reached and it's been unlocked. You'll discover Colt's Attack range and shooting speed increase by 11 percent automatically.

For 30 Gems (approximately $1.99 US), you're able to purchase the Rockstar Colt skin, which makes him look like Elvis, complete with black hair, sideburns, and an iconic white jumpsuit. Don't worry, Colt still hangs onto his pistols.

As you're targeting enemies using Six-Shooter, aim for where you anticipate your enemy is going to be by the time the bullets reach their destination. This is easier if the enemy is moving directly toward or away from you, but harder when the enemy is moving from side to side. Try to track and replicate an adversary's movements and rely on perfect timing to ensure Colt's shots hit their intended target. Of course, manually aiming the weapon will work nicely, but takes longer than using the auto-aiming feature.

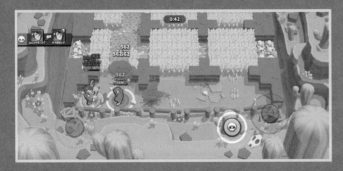

During the Big Game (Ticketed) match that's shown here, the Colt being controlled by JasonRich7 was the Big Brawler that five opposing brawlers needed to defeat. The big mistake made here was that Colt was pinned in the lower-left corner of the screen, so as multiple enemies attacked at once, there was little room for Colt to maneuver to avoid the incoming attacks. This caused a major drain to his Health meter. Pay attention to your surroundings and avoid getting pinned in a location where there's little or no room for movement. Having to travel directly toward an attacking enemy is rarely a good idea.

When you play one of the Events that allow you to team up with other gamers and you get matched up with random people, each time you're successful at winning a match consider sticking with those gamers and participating in additional matches. You'll be given the option to Play Again with the same partner or teammates. Within a few seconds after a match, select the Play Again option to do this. Otherwise, to get matched up with new allies, tap the Exit button, followed by the Play button.

Crow

Description	Some birds can fly, but Crow uses his legs to walk around the various arenas as he fights. When the need arises, he can leap into the air, but flying is just not this birdman's thing.
Rarity Classification	Legendary: This brawler appears randomly but rarely in Brawl Boxes, Big Boxes, or Mega Boxes. The more boxes you open, the better your chances he'll appear.
Brawler Type	Toxic Assassin

Crow is a birdman. His head looks like a bird, but his body appears to be humanoid. When he uses his Swoop Super capability, it has the potential to cause major damage if you use the manual aim feature and land directly on a target's head.

	Name	Description
Attack Capability	Switchblade	The birdman of **Brawl Stars** is able to throw three poison-tipped daggers at a time toward his enemies from a distance. As you'd expect, when one or more daggers hit their target, the recipient of the attack receives damage.
Super Capability	Swoop	While he can't exactly fly, when the Swoop attack is used, Crow leaps into the air and tosses a ring of his poison-tipped daggers down onto his enemies. In fact, daggers get thrown as he leaps up, and then again when he lands, giving him the opportunity to damage his enemy twice within a few seconds.
Star Power Capability	Extra Toxic	As soon as Crow reaches Power Level 9 and unlocks this ability, each time a poison dagger strikes an enemy, that enemy's ability to counterattack (or attack other enemies) temporarily becomes 10 percent weaker until the effect of the poison wears off.

Phoenix Crow and White Crow are two of the optional skins available for this brawler.

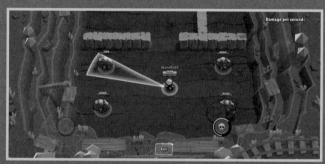

The three daggers that go flying when Crow uses his Switchblade attack spread out as they travel. Shown here, manual aiming is being used to target the Switchblade Attack. Notice the funnel shape of the white targeting tool. The far end shows the distance the daggers can reach, as well as their spread (the distance apart they'll be) when they get there.

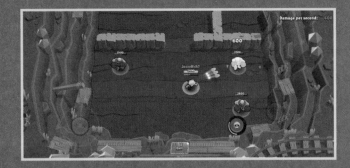

When they hit a close target, all three daggers will cause damage. However, the more the daggers spread out, the less likely it is that all three will hit the intended target. Shown here, the three daggers are traveling to their target (in this case, on the right side of the screen).

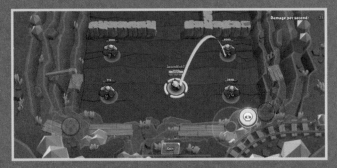

Once Crow's Super capability, Swoop, is fully charged, use manual aiming to target a specific enemy. Notice the arch shape of the targeting tool. This is because Crow will leap up, travel forwards, and then drop down on his target, assuming you aim correctly and use perfect timing.

Shown here, Swoop has been activated and Crow is airborne. He's about to land directly on top of an enemy's head (near the lower-left corner of the screen).

Crow works best from a distance. One opportune time to utilize Extra Toxic is when you are part of a team. Inflict some initial damage on an enemy from a distance, and then encourage your teammates to move in and finish the brawl while the enemy is poisoned.

Darryl

Description	If you ever wondered what would happen if you took a wooden barrel and transformed it into a fighting robot, when you see Darryl, you'll get your answer. He wears a pirate hat and carries two double-barrel shotguns, one in each hand.
Rarity Classification	Super Rare
Brawler Type	Heavyweight (Close-Range) Shooter

This is what Darryl looks like in his default skin. Shown here, he's been upgraded to Power Level 4, but is still at Rank 1.

	Name	Description
Attack Capability	Double Deuce	With each trigger pull, bullets shoot from Darryl's two shotguns. The closer he is to his enemies, the more damage his ammo will cause.
Super Capability	Barrel Roll	Darryl can pull his head and arms into his barrel (which is like a turtle's shell), and then roll toward his opponents to smash into them head-on. As he forces enemies to bounce backwards, Darryl can bounce off walls and solid objects while he's rolling around.
Star Power Capability	Steep Hoops	This move can be unlocked once Darryl reaches Power Level 9. When it's used, his wooden barrel becomes stronger, allowing him to withstand 30 percent more damage than usual for 3.5 seconds at a time. In other words, he can often survive even the most powerful incoming attack.

Darryl's Double Deuce Attack takes longer to recharge than the Attack capabilities of most other brawlers, so plan accordingly and use the three shots per charge wisely.

Double Deuce works best when only dealing with one nearby enemy at a time. Here, Darryl can be seen rolling towards his enemy after the Super capability was activated. You'll gain more of an advantage if you wait to use Barrel Roll until after you know the target has used up their Attack and/ or Super capability and is waiting helplessly for it to recharge.

Since Darryl needs to get in close to use Double Deuce and inflict the most damage possible, use his Barrel Roll as one way to quickly rush enemies. Here, the Double Duece is fully charged and is being manually aimed.

Regardless of which Brawler you're working with, invest the time needed to help them achieve Power Level 9 or higher. Once this happens, that brawler's Star Power capability becomes active. Practice using this newly acquired power so you discover how and when it can best be used to your utmost advantage during a brawl.

In summer 2019, Supercell introduced a bunch of new Star Power capabilities into the game—at least one for each brawler—so be sure to take advantage of them as they're unlocked and made available during matches.

Dynamike

Check out what Dynamike looks like when wearing his default skin.

Description	Dynamike may look like a jolly coal miner in his default skin, but in each hand he carries sticks of explosive dynamite used to blast away his enemies and whatever objects are in his path.
Rarity Classification	Unlock this brawler from Trophy Road by collecting 2,000 Trophies.
Brawler Type	Thrower: He can toss his dynamite a decent distance, which makes him great at long-range fighting.

	Name	Description
Attack Capability	Short Fuse	Not only can Dynamike toss two sticks of explosive dynamite at a time toward his enemies when he has a clear line of sight, but his dynamite can automatically be thrown over objects adversaries may be hiding behind. There's a little time between when the dynamite is tossed and when it explodes, so plan accordingly.
Super Capability	Big Barrel of Boom	Instead of just two sticks of dynamite exploding, when this attack is used, an even bigger explosion gets created. Dynamike can knock back enemies and cause them damage with his Big Barrel of Boom, plus destroy solid objects in the arena.
Star Power Capability	Dyna-Jump	As soon as Dynamike reaches Power Level 9 and unlocks this ability, he can ride the wave caused by his explosions and travel over obstacles in his path. Why waste time walking around solid objects when Dynamike can simply leap over them?

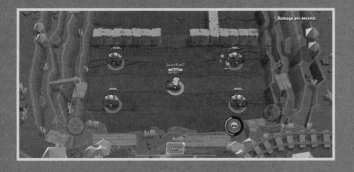

Dynamike's Short Fuse attack takes time to detonate. If an enemy spots the dynamite sticks before they explode, they can simply retreat to put distance between themselves and the blast zone. One way around this delay is to toss the dynamite as far from Dynamike as possible. The delayed detonation will start its countdown while the dynamite sticks are still airborne, so they explode almost instantly when they land. Shown here, Dynamike is using his Short Fuse Attack. He has thrown his dynamite at the bot located near the top-right corner of the screen.

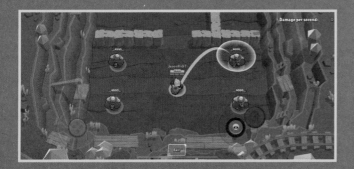

Manually aiming the Short Fuse attack helps guarantee the dynamite will land on its intended target.

One of the optional skins available for Dynamike resembles a chef's outfit. When wearing it, he trades in his dynamite sticks for red hot chili peppers that are also explosive.

El Primo

Description	If real-life WWE wrestlers could participate in **Brawl Stars**, they'd probably be no match for El Primo. He's a masked close-range brawler who's always wanting to pummel his opponents in the arena.
Rarity Classification	Rare
Brawler Type	Heavyweight: He's a close-range brawler.

To inflict the most damage, El Primo will often need to rush his enemies and then launch his Fists of Fury Attack once he's gotten close. Brawlers whom you know have powerful long-range Attack moves are more likely to be able to defend themselves from a distance when they notice El Primo approaching, so it's best for this brawler to sneak up on his targets whenever possible.

	Name	Description
Attack Capability	Fists of Fury	When El Primo uses his extra-large hands to make a fist and throw a punch, the brawler it lands on will feel the pain.
Super Capability	Flying Elbow Drop	Using his wrestling skills, El Primo leaps into the air and uses his elbow to smash an opponent or whatever solid object is below him.
Star Power Capability	El Fuego	Once El Primo reaches Power Level 9 and unlocks this ability, any time the Flying Elbow Drop is used, a fire will appear and enemies will receive 800HP worth of extra damage over the next four seconds. This move takes time to charge, but when used correctly, El Primo's enemies will get roasted, toasted, and defeated.

El Rudo Primo and El Rey Primo (which cost 80 gems each) are two of El Primo's optional skins. While they do change his appearance, he always keeps his pro wrestler persona. Remember, skins are used for cosmetic purposes only and do not impact a brawler's strength or capabilities during a match.

Shown here, El Primo is manually aiming his Attack at a chest in a Solo Showdown match. Notice the range for Fists of Fury is very short.

One easy mistake to make when controlling a brawler who specializes in close-range combat is that to start using their Attack move too soon, when you're not yet close enough to your opponent to do any damage. In this case, El Primo should have moved in closer before the Fists of Fury Attack move was used. Otherwise, it's a waste.

Frank

Description	Compared to other brawlers, Frank's name is pretty basic and common, but there's nothing ordinary about this brawler's fighting capabilities. In this case, Frank is short for Frankenstein. He's a muscled monster who specializes in close-range fighting. In his left hand, Frank carries a massive club.
Rarity Classification	Epic
Brawler Type	Heavyweight

The thing to remember about Frank's Hammer Hit is that it takes a half-second to charge before the shockwave forms. While the charging is taking place, Frank needs to stay still. For this attack to work well, position Frank so he's mid-range from his target. This is different from most brawlers, who carry weapons that can be shot instantly. Taking full advantage of Hammer Hit will require a bit of extra practice.

	Name	Description
Attack Capability	Hammer Hit	This fighting moves takes time to charge up, but once he's ready to swing his massive hammer, the shockwave will devastate any close-range enemies. You do not need to hit an enemy directly over the head using the hammer for this Attack to work. The shockwave created when the hammer hits the ground will damage any enemies who are nearby.
Super Capability	Stunning Blow	In addition to receiving damage with the strike of his hammer, nearby enemies will be temporarily stunned when this fighting move is used.
Star Power Capability	Power Grab	As soon as Frank reaches Power Level 9 and unlocks this ability, each time he defeats another, Frank steals some of their power. The result is that for the next 12 seconds, his attacks will be 50 percent stronger.

Any time Frank is part of a team and uses his Stunning Blow to temporarily stun enemies, it provides the perfect time for Frank's teammates to move in for an attack on those stunned brawlers. The drawback is that Stunning Blow takes time to charge up, during which the targeted enemies can retreat if they anticipate what's about to happen. Once enemies are stunned, Frank should have no trouble moving in close to use one Hammer Hit on them as well.

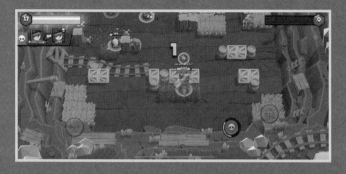

During this Gem Grab match, Frank managed to collect 15 Gems. To avoid losing them, he retreats back to his team's end of the arena, hides behind a wall and in a bush, and simply waits for the counter to reach zero . . . Match won!

One of the optional skins that Frank looks particularly good in is called Caveman Frank. Yup, he'll look like a purple-haired caveman.

It's easy to spot Frank when he's about to use his Hammer Hit attack because you can see the giant hammer being swung over his head as this move charges up. Perfect timing is essential when aiming at a target since there's a delay between when you activate this Attack and when it actually launches.

Gene

Description	Your wish is Gene's command. That is, unless you're his enemy and your wish is to survive a brawl. You guessed it: Gene is a magical genie with close- to mid-range fighting skill.
Rarity Classification	Mythic
Brawler Type	Support: In addition to holding his own in a brawl using magic, Gene is a skilled healer who can help his teammates stay alive longer during matches.

Gene is one of the brawlers you need to unlock by opening boxes. He'll appear randomly within a Brawl Box, for example, once he's good and ready.

Participating in Friendly Games is a great way to practice using a newly unlocked brawler, or their new Star Power once you unlock it. Any time you visit Training Cave, you'll compete against bots (computer-controlled adversaries). When you participate in a Friendly Game, you can test out your brawling skills against other human gamers, but you won't win or lose any Trophies or Tokens as a result of your efforts.

	Name	Description
Attack Capability	Smoke Blast	Like most genies, Gene carries a magical lamp. It shoots balls of toxic smoke. When one of these smoke balls hits its target, that brawler receives damage. However, when the smoke ball misses its target, a smoke cloud appears and any brawler caught in the cloud receives some damage, especially if they don't escape quickly.
Super Capability	Magic Hand	Gene has tiny hands, but using a bit of magic, a large and powerful hand will appear from his lamp and strike nearby enemies. The blow is often devastating.
Star Power Capability	Magic Puffs	In addition to working as a fighter, Gene is a skilled healer. When this move is used, any allies who are close by will receive a 200HP replenishment to their Health meter per second. With proper positioning, Gene can heal several teammates at once.

The trick when controlling a brawler that specializes in close- to mid-range attacks is being able to sneak up on enemies, especially if that enemy has a long-range weapon at their disposal and can see you approaching. Be sneaky and creative! Hide in bushes or behind objects, for example, to keep from being noticed.

Any time your brawler is hiding behind a wall, however, watch out for enemies with ammo that can travel over or through solid objects.

As you move around the arena, don't make a beeline for enemies you know have long-range weapons. Instead, follow an unpredictable zigzag pattern that will force the enemy to shoot their weapon frantically and hopefully miss you. Once their weapon needs to recharge, this gives you time to make a more direct approach—when they're vulnerable.

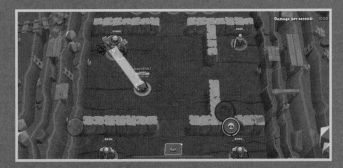

Shown here, Gene is manually aiming his Smoke Blast Attack.

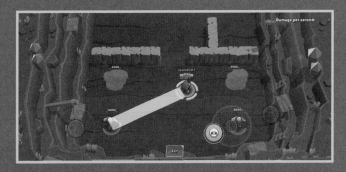

Gene's Magic Hand (his Super capability) can and should be manually aimed whenever possible. Notice it can only be aimed in a straight line.

Here's what the Magic Hand looks like when it's being shot at an enemy (in this case, near the lower-left corner of the screen).

Jessie

Description	With a smile on her face and her long red hair in ponytails, Jessie looks super friendly and totally harmless. Don't let her cute looks fool you, however. Jessie carries a rifle and she knows exactly how to use it!
Rarity Classification	Unlock this brawler from Trophy Road by collecting 500 Trophies.
Brawler Type	Fighter

Sure, Jessie's Shock Rifle is a useful weapon, but if you want to win matches controlling this brawler, you'll need to practice positioning her turret (Scrappy!), so it's able to target the most enemies possible. The location you place the turret is essential if you want it to cause significant damage and not quickly get destroyed by incoming attacks.

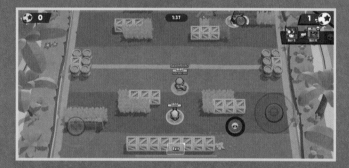

When fighting enemies that specialize in long-range brawling, place Scrappy! behind a wall to help protect it from long-range incoming attacks. However, when battling brawlers whom you know are great close-range brawlers, position Scrappy! out in the open. Shown here, Scrappy! has been placed behind Jessie, near the bottom-center of the screen.

	Name	Description
Attack Capability	Shock Rifle	From her rifle, Jessie is able to shoot energy orbs. After hitting one target, each orb can bounce around and then hit up to two additional nearby targets.
Super Capability	Scrappy!	In addition to her rifle, when the Scrappy! weapon is activated, a cannon-like turret appears in the arena and will automatically target and shoot at enemies until it's destroyed by enemy attacks. The turret has its own Health meter. Its capacity expands as Jessie's Power Level increases.
Star Power Capability	Energize	Once Jessie reaches Power Level 9 and unlocks this ability, she can repair her own turret (if it has received enemy damage) and increase its Health meter by 800HP by hitting it with her Shock Rifle attack.

One optional skin available to Jessie is called Dragon Knight Jessie. It allows her to dress up like a knight and her turret gets disguised as a dragon.

Jessie is easily maneuverable when traveling around an arena, and she can attack enemies from a good distance. Shown here, her Shock Rifle Attack capability is being manually aimed.

Another of Jessie's optional skins is called Summer Jessie. In this outfit, she looks like she's planning a fun day at the beach. Her rifle resembles a Super Soaker® water gun and her turret looks like a yellow rubber duck.

While taking part in a Brawl Ball match within the Backyard Bowl arena. Jessie grabbed ahold of the ball, traveled quickly toward the opposing side's goal, and scored the match-winning point.

Leon

Description	Inside his bright-colored hoodie is a lollipop-eating boy who seems rather meek. That is, until Leon steps into the arena. This is when he transforms into a stealthy assassin.
Rarity Classification	Legendary
Brawler Type	Assassin

Leon is one of the brawlers you'll eventually unlock by opening up boxes. His appearance in a box will be random. Since Leon is considered a Legendary brawler, each time you open a Big Box or Mega Box, for example, the chance of unlocking a Legendary brawler (which could be Leon) is just 0.1104 percent, so when he appears in a box, consider yourself lucky!

If you use Smoke Bomb while Leon is out in the open and an enemy is watching closely, it's still sometimes possible to track his movements. However, if Leon is hiding in a bush and out of sight, and then uses his Smoke Bomb, he can temporarily travel more freely around the arena without being detected.

	Name	Description
Attack Capability	Spinner Blades	From his hoodie's pockets, Leon whips out four spinning blades and throws them at enemies. While most brawlers with a projectile weapon make better long-distance fighters, this is *not* the case for Leon. The farther his sharp blades travel before reaching their target, the less damage they'll cause. This makes Leon more useful in close- or mid-range attacks.
Super Capability	Smoke Bomb	When used, Leon becomes almost (but not completely) invisible for seven seconds. Enemies who are close will be able to spot him if they look carefully. Using this capability, Leon can sneak up on enemies to use his Spinner Blades, or make it difficult for enemies to follow him when he needs to make a hasty retreat.
Star Power Capability	Smoke Trails	Once Leon reaches Power Level 9 and then unlocks this ability, any time he uses a Smoke Bomb (his Super capability), he's able to travel faster while he's practically invisible (for about seven seconds).

Any time you're confronted by an enemy that specializes in long-range attacks and you're still at a good distance from them, make them think you're going to run in a straight line toward them so they shoot their weapon and use it up. Since you're at a distance, you'll see the weapon's ammo approaching and will have time to quickly dodge it. Once you know the enemy is vulnerable, move in to launch your own attack.

Mortis

Description	Is he a superhero or a vampire? You'll have to decide for yourself when you control Mortis or must brawl against him in an arena. For his weapon, Mortis carries a shovel with a sharp edge that can be used to slice and dice his enemies.
Rarity Classification	Mythic
Brawler Type	Dashing Assassin

This is what Mortis looks like when wearing his default skin.

Mortis was unlocked after taking advantage of a Daily Deal from the Shop that promoted that a random Mystic brawler could be unlocked instantly for 350 Gems (approximately $19 US).

	Name	Description
Attack Capability	Shovel Swing	Each time the Attack button is pressed and this attack move is charged up, Mortis will rush his opponent, and at the same time swing his shovel to cause some damage.
Super Capability	Life Blood	Mortis is able to summon a swarm of vampire bats that'll literally suck the life out of nearby enemies. At the same time, Mortis is able to recharge is own Health meter, which makes him even harder to defeat.
Star Power Capability	Creepy Harvest	Any time Mortis defeats an enemy, he's able to suck their life energy and use it to recharge his own Health meter by up to 1,400HP. To use this power, however, Mortis must first achieve Power Level 9 and unlock this ability.

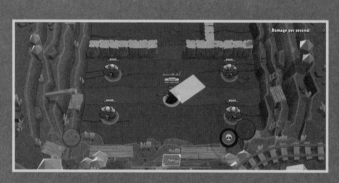

The Shovel Attack has a very short range, as you can see here, when manual aiming is being used and the targeting tool is displayed. It's best to manually aim the Shovel Swing attack so you specifically target enemies when you need to. If you rely on automatic aiming and there's a wall or solid object nearby, you may wind up smashing that object as opposed to attacking the enemy. Only use auto-aiming when there are no nearby objects that could take the brunt of the attack instead of the intended enemy.

Top Hat Mortis is one of the optional skins available for this brawler. It's a bit more formal than his usual attire.

Rockability is the name of another optional skin available to Mortis. He still keeps his vampire-like appearance and purple hair, but his outfit looks like something Elvis Presley might have worn back in the day.

When Mortis throws on this optional outfit, called Night Witch Mortis, he transforms into a powerful female witch.

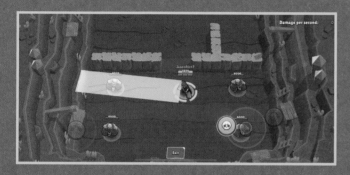

Unlike his Shovel Swing Attack, when Mortis uses his Life Blood Super capability, it works very well from a distance. Shown here is the aiming tool being used to demonstrate how far this Super capability can reach.

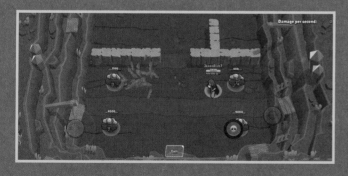

Once Life Blood is launched, you'll see the swarm of bats flying quickly at their target.

Nita

Description	Nita comes from a remote island. She's rather small in size but is able to conjure up her extra-large best friend on demand. He happens to be a giant red bear capable of tearing apart enemies. Nita and her companion are highly skilled fighters at close range, mid range, or from a distance.
Rarity Classification	Unlock this brawler from Trophy Road by collecting just 10 Trophies.
Brawler Type	Fighter

Because Nita's Attack can pass through walls, she should use walls to her advantage and stay protected behind them as much as possible.

	Name	Description
Attack Capability	Rupture	Using magical capabilities, Nita is able to create a powerful shockwave and send it from her hands toward her rivals. Anyone who gets caught in the wave receives damage.
Super Capability	Overbearing	Any time Nita summons Big Baby Bear (an oversized red bear), he will hunt down and attack enemies on his own, using his claws. Big Baby Bear has a separate Health Meter from Nita.
Star Power Capability #1	Bear With Me	Once Nita reaches Power Level 9 and unlocks this ability, any time Big Baby Bear defeats an enemy, Nita's Health meter automatically recovers up to 500HP. Meanwhile, any time Nita is able to defeat an enemy on her own, Big Baby Bear's Health meter, which is separate from Nita's, will be replenished by up to 500HP. When the two work together, they're able to keep each other alive longer during matches.
Star Power Capability #2	Hyper Bear	This second Star Power also kicks in once Power Level 9 has been reached and it's been unlocked. Big Baby Bear's attacks occur faster and its recharge time is 50 percent faster.

Nita loves bears. Any type of bears. When she throws on her optional Panda Nita skin (price: 30 Gems), she gets to wear a panda costume while Big Baby Bear gets transformed into an oversized panda.

Shiba Nita (price: 150 Gems) is another of Nita's optional skins. As you can see, it too transforms her appearance, as well as what Big Baby Bear looks like.

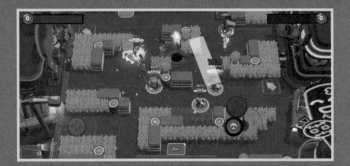

Use Nita's targeting tool to aim her Rupture attack. It's capable of traveling a decent range toward an enemy.

Nita's ability to summon Big Baby Bear is what makes this brawler extremely useful during many brawls, since once this oversized bear enters the arena, he'll go off on his own to attack enemies. You can see Nita and Big Baby Bear near the center of the screen. Big Baby Bear is attacking an enemy during a Solo Showdown match. If you're in a Duo match, by summoning Big Baby Bear, your partnership will now become a threesome, giving you an advantage over the opposing team. Likewise, if you're playing a 3 vs 3 Event, summoning Big Baby Bear adds a fourth member to your team, making it stronger and harder to defeat.

Pam

Description	It's impossible to confuse Jessie with Pam, although they both have bright red hair. Pam is larger, more muscular, and looks much meaner. However, in addition to being a skilled fighter, Pam is also a healer. She can nicely round out the capabilities of a three-brawler team when her two teammates are both fighters.
Rarity Classification	Epic
Brawler Type	Healer

Each time Pam's Scrapstorm is used, nine projectiles are shot out at once. Two go to the left. Two travel a bit to the right. Five, however, travel straight. Knowing this, you'll cause more damage to enemies when you manually aim the attack and try to ensure at least five projectiles hit your intended target.

	Name	Description
Attack Capability	Scrapstorm	On her back, Pam carries a weird-looking contraption that shoots scrap metal shrapnel at her enemies. Each time one of these metal pieces hits an enemy, they take some damage.
Super Capability	Mama's Kiss	When activated, a healing turret appears near Pam. As long as her partner or teammates stay in close proximity to it, their Health meter will replenish more every second. The healing turret has its own Health meter, which gets depleted as enemies attack it.
Star Power Capability	Mama's Hug	Each time Pam uses Scrapstorm and hits an enemy, her own Health meter, as well as the Health meters of her nearby partner or teammates, will get a 30HP boost. For this to work, however, Pam must first reach Power Level 9 and unlock this ability.

Pam's Scrapstorm has a good range, which makes her easier to control compared to other brawlers. She's a good match for newbs or gamers who want to fight but also can serve as a healer in battle.

Mama's Kiss can be placed anywhere in the arena once it's been charged up by first launching a bunch of successful attacks using Scrapstorm. The large green ring has a healing turret inside. It only works on Pam and her teammates, as long as they stand in the ring. Place the turret in an area that's less prone to enemy attacks. Dead-center of the arena (shown here) is not the most strategic location to place it.

Because Pam's Scrapstorm spreads out as it travels toward enemies, this Attack works really well against multiple enemies standing close together.

In addition to regular Events that can be unlocked throughout the week, don't ignore the opportunity to participate in Ticketed Events. To gain entry to these weekend-only Events, you'll first need to collect Tickets. Tickets are available from boxes or can be purchased from the Shop, for example. Each time you access the Choose Event screen to unlock Ticketed Events, you'll automatically receive two free Tickets.

As a newb, to participate in Ticketed Events, you'll first need to collect a total of 350 Trophies and reach the Ticketed Events milestone along Trophy Road. Once Ticketed Events are unlocked, there will be a different challenge each weekend. Shown here, Pam is about to participate in a Big Game Ticketed Event. By looking at the Play icon, you can see the admission price is one Ticket, and by looking near the top-center of the screen, you can see that this gamer has 31 Tickets available.

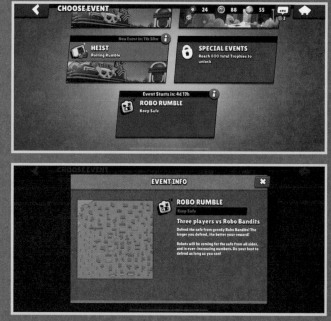

On weekdays, when you access the Choose Event screen, a preview of the next Ticketed Event, along with a timer that shows when it'll become active, is displayed. Shown here, Robo Rumble will automatically unlock in 4 days and 17 hours. In the meantime, tap the Info ("i") icon in the top-right corner of the Robo Rumble banner to see a preview of what this Ticketed Event is all about.

Penny

Description	You'd think Penny's pistol would be her main weapon, but you'd be wrong. Her pouch filled with fool's gold allows her to dole out damage. Penny is a skilled long-range brawler with plenty of attitude. Her career goal is to be a world-class pirate, so she brings along her very own cannon whenever she enters an arena.
Rarity Classification	Super Rare
Brawler Type	Sharpshooter

This is the Home screen with Penny selected as the active brawler.

	Name	Description
Attack Capability	Plunderbuss	From her shoulder pouch, Penny tosses out chunks of fool's gold, which look like gold coins. When the coins hit enemies, her targets receive damage, not riches.
Super Capability	Old Lobber	When Penny sets up her cannon, it will automatically shoot at enemies even if they're at a distance or they're hiding behind a solid object. The cannon has its own health meter and causes damage with each cannonball that hits its target.
Star Power Capability	Last Blast	Knowing Penny's cannon poses a threat to her enemies, it makes sense that they'll try to destroy it at the same time they try to defeat Penny during brawls. Once Penny reaches Power Level 9 and unlocks this ability, any time the cannon is about to be destroyed in battle, it'll automatically launch one final cluster of bombs, each of which will cause mega-damage to those unfortunate brawlers who get caught in the blast zone.

To take full advantage of Old Lobber, position it in an arena in the most advantageous location possible. It can then keep shooting enemies automatically while Penny uses Plunderbuss to manually target her shots. The combination of Plunderbuss Attacks with incoming fire from Old Lobber should prove fatal to many enemy brawlers. As you can see here, Penny is standing close to the Old Lobber she placed near the center of the screen.

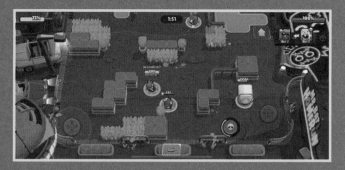

During this Heist match, Penny is standing above and slightly to the left of the Old Lobber she placed in the arena. Its location will help ward off enemies who approach her team's safe from the left.

While Penny's default outfit looks sort of menacing, it's harder to take her seriously when she puts on the Bunny Penny outfit, available as an optional skin (priced at 80 Gems). Whenever she struts this outfit, she looks like a giant pink rabbit with a sinister attitude. Other skins for Penny can occasionally be acquired using Star Points.

Penny's Plumberbuss Attack can be manually aimed using the targeting tool. As you can see, this weapon can only be shot in a straight line, but it has a really good range.

Piper

Description	Being a princess, Piper expects everyone she encounters to bow down before her. Those that don't, well, they get pummeled. That pink umbrella Piper carries is not to protect to her from the sun or rain. It's a lethal weapon that can defeat enemies from a distance.
Rarity Classification	Epic
Brawler Type	Sharpshooter

If you're a skilled gamer who chooses to control Piper, with a bit of practice you can expect most battles to have a fairytale ending.

Piper's Gunbrella takes extra time to reload, so you'll get the most use out of this weapon if you manually aim it as opposed to using the auto-aiming feature. Try to conserve at least one of the three rounds of ammo in case an enemy gets too close or needs some extra attention to defeat them. Manually shooting, as opposed to automatic aiming, often works best when controlling Piper.

	Name	Description
Attack Capability	Gunbrella	Unlike some projectile weapons in *Brawl Stars* that become weaker the farther the ammunition travels, the shots from Piper's parasol (umbrella) become more powerful the farther they travel before hitting their target.
Super Capability	Poppin'	When Piper uses her Poppin' powers, she leaps out of harm's way and leaves behind some explosive grenades designed to blow away those who oppose her.
Star Power Capability	Ambush	Once Piper reaches Power Level 9 and unlocks this ability, each time she shoots her Gunbrella while hiding in a bush, each direct hit will cause 400HP extra damage on the enemies she hits.

One way to collect Power Points is to receive them from Brawl Boxes, Big Boxes, or Mega Boxes. The goal with Power Points is to upgrade your brawlers to at least Power Level 9, so each can unlock and use their unique Star Power capabilities.

After you've been playing *Brawl Stars* for a while, you'll eventually upgrade all the brawlers to Power Level 9 or 10. Once you do this, instead of receiving Power Points from boxes, you'll receive extra Coins instead.

Shown here (below the Daily Deals heading, in the bottom-left slot), 12 additional Power Points could be purchased specifically for Piper at a cost of 24 Coins. However, for 39 Gems (about $3 US), the day's Special Offer could be purchased. In this case, the offer included a bundle of 220 Power Points that could be assigned to any brawler.

Poco

Description	This Mexican brawler wears a sombrero and uses music as a weapon, although when he's part of a team, Poco can serve as a healer as well. His main weapon is a *guitarrón* (a musical instrument) that uses sound waves to inflict harm and dole out damage.
Rarity Classification	Rare
Brawler Type	Healer

Poco is a perfect brawler to control if you're a newb, mainly because when he uses his Power Chord attack, it covers a wide area, so manually aiming is far less important than it is when controlling other brawlers. When Poco is facing just one enemy at a time, don't waste valuable time aiming. Just use the Power Chord to launch attacks. Aiming is important, however, if you plan to use Da Capo! to heal one or more teammates who are nearby.

Some expert **Brawl Stars** gamers consider Poco to be one of the weaker brawlers overall, so as you expand your gaming skills and gain practice, you might want to move onto controlling other brawlers.

	Name	Description
Attack Capability	Power Chord	A few strums on his *guitarrón* and the sound waves Poco creates can be lethal to the brawlers close enough to hear it. Musical note icons depict the range the audible damage will reach.
Super Capability	Encore	Any time Poco changes his tune and plays a special melody, he's able to heal himself and his partner or teammates who are nearby. This ability has no positive or negative impact on his enemies, however. When controlling Poco, pay attention to where your teammates are at all times, so you can step in to heal them when they need it most. As a healer, keeping your teammates strong is often more important than going on the offensive to defeat enemies yourself during a match.
Star Power Capability	Da Capo!	Once Poco reaches Power Level 9 and unlocks this ability, when he uses his Power Chord attack on allies, they'll get a 500HP boost to their Health meter. That should help them withstand some powerful enemy attacks and keep them in the match a bit longer.

Poco keeps his Mexican outfit looking authentic no matter which optional skin he uses. The Serenade Poco skin (price: 150 Gems), for example, changes up the outfit's color scheme and showcases a more lovable look.

Even without manually aiming, Poco's Power Chord can strike multiple enemies at once who are close together. It's important to remember, however, that Poco works best when he keeps his distance from enemies.

By activating the manual targeting tool, you can see that Power Chord can cover a widespread area. Unfortunately, Poco's Power Chord is one of the weakest Attack capabilities in the game, but on the plus side, it recharges very quickly. It's this brawler's healing skills that make him valuable as part of a multi-brawler team. You'll likely discover that Poco performs better in Events like Gem Grab and Brawl Ball, as opposed to Bounty or Heist.

Thanks to Power Chord's quick reload time, it's usually a good idea to keep firing until the attack is drained, fall back for a few seconds to recharge, and then move in again to attack the closest adversaries.

Using the manual targeting tool for Encore, you can see this Super capability can reach a far distance, plus cover a widespread area with each shot.

Once Encore is fully charged and activated, a massive soundwave that looks like a moving green cloud shoots from Poco's guitarrón. It's seen here near the top-right corner of the screen.

Rico

Description	Not all brawlers are created equal. In fact, some aren't even human. Rico is a high-tech robot with a colorful personality and some power-packed fighting moves.
Rarity Classification	Super Rare
Brawler Type	Sharpshooter

If you choose to control Rico (short for Ricochet), practice manually aiming Rico's weapon so you can successfully and consistently bounce the bullets off walls and other solid objects.

*Become skilled at hitting targets from around corners. Learning to control bouncing bullets is one of the hardest skills to master in **Brawl Stars**, but once you do, you'll often find yourself enjoying a tactical advantage. When aiming the Bouncy Bullets Attack, notice the aiming tool can go in a straight line or you can aim it from an angle at a wall and the trajectory of the bullets will bounce around.*

	Name	Description
Attack Capability	Bouncy Bullets	Rico carries a futuristic-looking pistol that shoots bouncing bullets. This ammo can bounce off solid walls and ricochet toward an enemy, even when they're hiding behind a solid object.
Super Capability	Trick Shot	When Trick Shot is used, Rico's weapon shoots an extended burst of ammo. It'll blow right through enemies, bounce off walls, and ricochet into additional nearby enemies. In other words, one attack can take out multiple opponents if they're close together and Rico aims properly.
Star Power Capability #1	Super Bouncy	Any time Rico's bouncing bullets first bounce off a solid object and then hit a target, they'll inflict an extra 100HP worth of damage. This starts once Rico reaches Power Level 9 and unlocks the Super Bouncy capability.
Star Power Capability #2	Robo Retreat	This second Star Power also kicks in once Power Level 9 has been reached and it's been unlocked. When Rico's Health meter drops to below 40 percent, he's able to run 34 percent faster.

No matter what Rico wears, he can't conceal the fact that he's a robot. However, the Loaded Rico skin (price: 150 Gems) makes him look like royalty, while the Popcorn Rico skin allows him to brawl while simultaneously popping up some fresh movie theater-style popcorn.

Remember, there are more than eight different types of Events that can be unlocked in *Brawl Stars*, and each Event type can feature one of several different arena designs. (You'll only experience one at a time.)

If you want to change things up and focus your skills on overcoming a different set of challenges, switch to playing a different Event. Each day, the first time you unlock and win an Event, you'll receive one Star Token. Redeem 10 Star Tokens to be able to open a Big Box and benefit from all of the goodies you receive as a result.

This Home screen shows Rico has been selected. If you look in the bottom-left corner of the screen, four out of the required 10 Star Tokens have already been collected. Plus, if you look near the top-left corner of the screen, you can see that another Trophy Road milestone has been reached. This is indicated by the yellow icon (with a red and white star in the corner of it).

Rosa

Description	As a botanist, Rosa studies plants and loves working with them. Her research, however, has taught her to use plants to defeat her enemies, especially when they're at close range.
Rarity Classification	Rare
Brawler Type	Heavyweight

Rosa's Hands of Stone allow her to quickly throw up to three punches in quick succession. If each hits a target, she'll inflict a lot of damage, but she'll need to be really close to her opponents to achieve this.

	Name	Description
Attack Capability	Hands of Stone	Using her fists, Rosa is able to launch some powerful one-two punches that'll knock the HP right out of her opponent when they're struck at close range.
Super Capability	Strong Stuff	When she needs shielding from an incoming attack, using her Strong Stuff capability, Rosa is able to instantly grow a protective vine around her body. For three seconds, this vine will reduce the impact of an incoming attack by 70 percent.
Star Power Capability #1	Plant Life	Once she reaches Power Level 9 and unlocks this capability, any time Rosa hides in a bush in any arena, her Health meter recovers 200HP per second until it's fully recharged.
Star Power Capability #2	Thorny Gloves	This second Star Power also kicks in once Power Level 9 has been reached and it's been unlocked. While using her Strong Stuff move, Rosa's punches cause 200HP more damage.

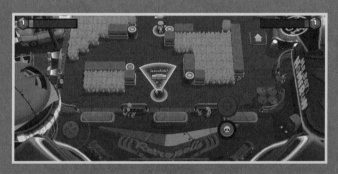

As you can see by activating Rosa's targeting tool for her Strong Stuff Attack, its range is very limited.

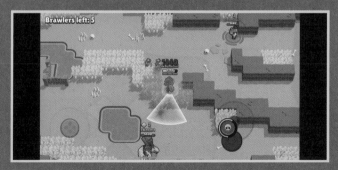

Instead of trying to rush enemies in order to get close, try hiding in a bush and waiting for an enemy to approach and walk within range of Rosa's Strong Stuff Attack, and then quickly launch all three rounds directly at the close-up enemy. This becomes more of a timing challenge than an accurate aiming challenge.

Thanks to the extra shielding Rosa's Strong Stuff capability provides, when it's used correctly it could require an enemy to launch up to 12 direct attacks before Rosa's Health meter hits zero. This gives her a lot of staying power during a tough match.

With a bit of practice to overcome the limited range of her Hands of Stone Attack capability, you too can control this brawler, win matches, and achieve the Star Player title.

Make sure you understand the main objective(s) for whichever Event type you're currently experiencing. If you're playing Gem Grab, for example, the main goal is to collect Gems, not necessarily defeat enemy brawlers. When playing a Solo or Duo Showdown Event, the objective is to defeat enemies, although allowing enemies to defeat each other while you bust open chests will reduce the number of opponents your brawler will need to fight. Any time you're playing a Bounty event, the objective is to find and grab Stars. Focus on defeating the enemies carrying around the most stars to reap the best reward.

Shelly

Description	She's young, energetic, and one heck of a well-rounded brawler, which is why she's the first brawler you'll unlock when you first start playing *Brawl Stars*. Shclly uscs a pistol as a primary weapon. Although this is a projectile weapon, her brawling skills work well from any distance.
Rarity Classification	She's the brawler all gamers start off with by default. As you start playing *Brawl Stars*, invest the time needed to build up her Power Level. Having at least one nicely upgraded brawler you know how to control well can be a huge advantage, especially when playing matches in which you're teamed up with random gamers.
Brawler Type	Fighter

Shelly is one of the most well-rounded brawlers in the game. She's good at brawling from any distance, and has Attack, Super, and Star Power capabilities that'll hold their own against any enemy when used correctly.

	Name	Description
Attack Capability	Buckshot	Shelly's pistol shoots ammo that inflicts the most damage at mid range. Since the ammo breaks into multiple pellets, the more pellets that hit each target, the more damage they'll cause. In other words, this works best as a close- to mid-range weapon.
Super Capability	Super Shell	When Shelly uses this super-powered ammo in her pistol, it'll destroy solid objects, inflict extra damage on enemies, plus send them flying backwards if they're not defeated by the ammo strikes.
Star Power Capability #1	Shell Shock	As soon as Shelly reaches Power Level 9 and unlocks this capability, each time she uses her pistol's Super Shell ammo, it'll slow her target down for three seconds and cause some damage.
Star Power Capability #2	Band-Aid	This second Star Power also kicks in once Power Level 9 has been reached and it's been unlocked. When Shelly's Health meter goes below 40 percent, she instantly and automatically returns to 100 percent Health. This power takes 20 seconds to recharge between uses.

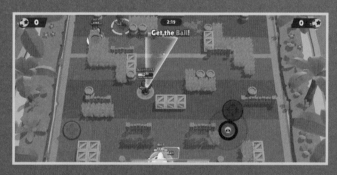

While Shelly's default appearance does not make her look too tough, switching to the Bandita Shelly skin, which includes a bandanna and eye patch, makes her appear a bit tougher and more intimidating.

Because her capabilities are so well rounded, Shelly is the perfect brawler to control if you're a newb. At first, you can rely on the weapon's auto-targeting capability when using Buckshot, but as you get more comfortable in the arena, practice manually aiming the weapon directly at specific adversaries.

Spike

Description	**Brawl Stars** features brawlers that are humans, robots, mummies, monsters, and vampires. There's even a fighting cactus, appropriately named Spike.
Rarity Classification	Legendary
Brawler Type	Sharpshooter

After achieving a bunch of direct hits using Buckshot, Shelly's Super Shell will get charged up and be ready for action. Just like with all the brawlers, when her Super is fully charged, the Shoot icon near the bottom-right corner of the screen will turn yellow. In addition to being a more powerful weapon, notice that its spread is almost double the width as that of the Buckshot, so you can potentially damage multiple enemies positioned close together.

Spike's Needle Grenade has a slow recharge time, but each shot can pack a wallop. Knowing this, manually aim your shots whenever possible, and launch one shot at a time as opposed to all three in quick succession. Once Spike uses up his shots and needs to wait for a recharge, he's very vulnerable. This could place him in jeopardy if he gets stuck in a close-range fight with no shots remaining. Conservation of ammo is key!

	Name	Description
Attack Capability	Needle Grenade	From his body, Spike shoots out a mini cactus. While it is airborne, sharp spikes go flying in all directions and cause damage to any brawlers that get hit.
Super Capability	Stick Around	Instead of a small cactus that shoots spikes, when Stick Around is used, Spike throws an exploding grenade at his target. Any enemies in the blast zone receive damage, plus they're temporarily slowed down.
Star Power Capability	Fertilize	Once Spike uses his Stick Around attack, if he stays in the blast zone he created, his own Health meter will replenish by 500HP per second until the meter is fully charged or the blast dissipates.

Who says a cactus must be green? When Spike throws on the Sakura Spike skin, he turns light pink. Don't worry, his attacks remain just as dangerous.

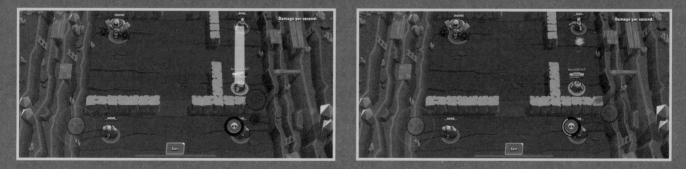

Spike's Needle Grenade can be manually aimed or shot using the auto-aiming feature. Either way, it can reach a good distance, and the ammo (sharp cactus spikes that look like a blue sphere when flying through the air) always travels in a straight line.

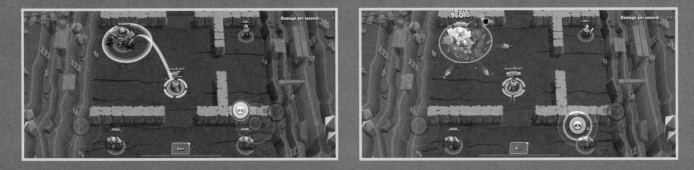

Spike's Stick Around Super capability works best when you manually aim the attack. Notice the aiming tool features a curved trajectory. Once the weapon lands, the blue circle around the enemy represents the blast zone. As long as the enemy stays within it, they receive additional 500HP damage every second. During an intense battle, if you don't notice when Spike's Super has fully charged, you could accidently launch it instead of using his regular Attack. Watch for the Fire button to turn yellow and then take advantage of the Super to dole out more damage.

Tara

Description	Brawling can be an intense activity, but Tara refuses to get wrapped up in the drama. Instead, as a mummy, she wraps herself in colorful bandages and is able to use tarot cards to see the future. For her enemies, more often than not, the future looks rather dim. Tara is one of the more unusual brawlers in the game, but not one of the more powerful ones.
Rarity Classification	Mythic
Brawler Type	Skirmisher

Tara's Gravity move is what can set her apart during a match and help you achieve victory. The Triple Tarot is useful, but not as powerful as the Attack capabilities of other brawlers. Perhaps focus on launching the Gravity move, and then use Triple Tarot again as a quick follow-up if you need to finish off an opponent.

	Name	Description
Attack Capability	Triple Tarot	Instead of using her tarot cards to read the future of her adversaries, she flicks three cards at a time at her targets and slashes them with razor-like precision.
Super Capability	Gravity	Using her powerful mind, Tara is able to lift two or more enemies into the air and force them to crash together, inflicting damage on multiple brawlers at the same time. Of course, for this to work properly, two or more of her enemies need to be in close proximity to each other and to her.
Star Power Capability	Black Portal	Two Taras fighting together are always more powerful than just one. Once Tara reaches Power Level 9 and unlocks this capability, any time she uses her Black Portal move, a darker clone of her appears in the arena and immediately begins attacking nearby enemies.

When you manually aim the Triple Tarot, you can see its reach is pretty good, but the flying tarot cards spread out as they fly toward their target.

Once the Triple Tarot is launched, you'll see the three blue tarot cards flying through the air toward their target.

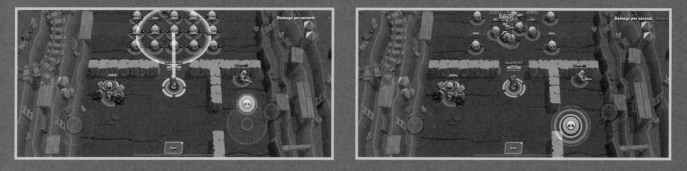

Tara's Super capability, Gravity, works best when used against multiple enemies standing in close proximity. You'll get three shots with each re-charge, each of which will crash the enemies together and inflict damage, especially when aimed strategically. When multiple enemies are clustered, manually aim Gravity toward the center of the group.

Remember, by collecting Trophies you'll be able to advance along Trophy Road and win prizes. Each time you win a match (or achieve specific objectives within certain Events), you'll win a pre-determined number of Trophies.

A Brawler's individual Trophy count determines their Rank. Shown here, Tara is only at Rank 1 and requires five additional Trophies to advance to Rank 2. As you'll discover, Rank is different from a brawler's Power Level, which impacts the capacity of their Health meter, as well as how much power their Attack and Super capabilities have.

Tick

Description	A bouncing round robot with long-range fighting capabilities.
Rarity Classification	Unlock this brawler from Trophy Road by collecting 4,000 Trophies.
Brawler Type	Thrower

*On June 25, 2019, as part of the company's **Brawl Talk** YouTube video (https://youtu.be/ s54bsh0OOu4), Supercell announced plans to add a new brawler named Tick into the game as brawler #27. He became unlockable the following day.*

Tick is a shiny robot with a removable head. He's been described by the folks at Supercell as "a metal ball made up of barely containable energy." This robot's specialty is causing explosions. To unlock him, you'll need to collect 4,000 Trophies, which even for the best gamers, will take a lot of time.

	Name	Description
Attack Capability	Minimines	It looks like Tick tosses just one explosive at a time, but while it's in midair, it separates into three separate explosive mines, each of which can cause damage on its own. One of the mines will detonate as soon as an enemy steps on it, or they'll all automatically explode a few seconds after they land on the ground.
Super Capability	Headfirst	Tick can remove his head and throw it around the arena. The flying head will automatically be attracted to a nearby enemy, and when it makes contact, it'll explode.
Star Power Capability	Well Oiled	Once this Star Power capability is unlocked (after reaching Power Level 9), each time Tick receives damage but does not launch a counterattack right away, he begins replenishing his Heath meter two seconds faster than normal.

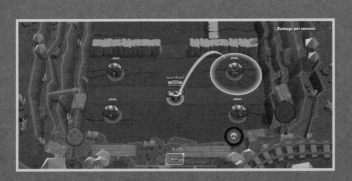

When manually aiming Minimines, the targeting tool uses a rounded trajectory since the mines get tossed up into the air and then come falling down around the target. This Attack is a superb long-distance explosive weapon.

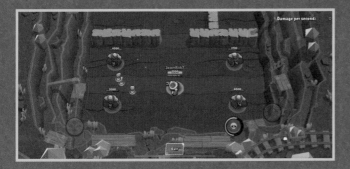

While in midair, the one mine will break apart into three separate Minimines, which will land slightly apart from each other.

Notice that when Headfirst is charged up and you try to manually aim the robot's exploding head, the distance it can travel is much shorter than the Minimines Attack. Thus, to create the biggest bang possible, Tick will need to move in close, launch the Super attack, and the retreat to a safe distance from which he can launch more Minimines Attacks.

More Brawlers Are Always On the Way

Every so often, Supercell (the developer of **Brawl Stars**) releases new brawlers. When this happens, it's announced within the game's News section. As these new characters are introduced into the game, discover what their unique capabilities are, and then determine how to acquire or unlock them.

What to Expect From New Brawlers

Each brawler introduces a new way to fight during matches, which means you'll need to practice using their unique Attack, Super, and Star Power moves and figure out when they should be used to round out the overall offensive and defensive capabilities of a multi-brawler team, when applicable.

To keep *Brawl Stars* well balanced, Supercell periodically increases or decreases the power and capabilities of some brawlers (or their individual Attack, Super, and/or Star Power capabilities). This is referred to as "balancing" or "rebalancing" their capabilities. When this happens, it's featured in the game's News section. Any time one or more of a brawler's capabilities are made weaker, it's referred to as getting "nerfed."

Unlock Brawler Skins and Upgrade Your Brawlers

Brawler skins can be unlocked and collected randomly from boxes or purchased. While these don't alter a brawler's offensive or defensive capabilities, they do allow you to change their appearance.

To purchase or use an unlocked skin, follow these steps:

Step #1: *From the Home screen, tap the Brawlers icons.*

Step #2: *Tap the desired brawler you've previously unlocked, whose appearance you want to change using a skin available to you.*

Step #3: *When the selected brawler's profile screen is displayed, on the left side of the screen, tap the "<" or ">" arrow icon to scroll between available skins. When you see a question mark icon over a skin slot, this means it's not yet available to you.*

Step #4: *If a skin is available for purchase, its price will be displayed in a yellow Buy button. Tap this button to buy it using Gems. In this case, the El Rey Primo Skin for El Primo can be purchased for 80 Gems (about $4.99 US).*

Step #5: *Confirm your in-app purchase decision by tapping the green Price button, which in this case says 80 Gems.*

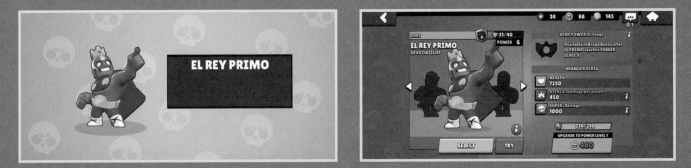

Step #6: *After making the purchase, tap the Select button to choose the skin and apply it to the brawler.*

Step #7: *You'll be returned to the Home screen, and the selected brawler will be wearing the newly acquired Skin.*

Starting in summer 2019, Star Points were introduced into **Brawl Stars** as a new type of in-game currency that can be used to acquire exclusive skins and other items for your brawlers. Keep in mind: Whether they are won, purchased using Gems, or acquired using Star Points, skins do *not* impact a brawler's fighting capabilities or defensive strength. These upgrades are for cosmetic purposes only.

SECTION 4

35 BRAWL STAR STRATEGIES FOR NEWBS

This section offers a collection of tips and strategies to use when playing all the different Events featured in *Brawl Stars*. Some of the strategies are useful only during a specific type of Event, in a particular arena, or when controlling a certain brawler, so take advantage of what applies to the challenges you're facing during any given match.

#1—There Are Two Ways to Practice Your Brawling Skills

Spending time in the Training Cave with a selected brawler or participating in a Friendly Game are two ways to gain practice playing *Brawl Stars* and, over time, improve your skills with no negative consequences for losing or getting defeated.

Any time you want to check out the unique capabilities of a brawler firsthand, one easy way to do this is to tap the Brawlers icon from the Home screen, select any of the brawlers (whether you've previously unlocked them or not), and then from a brawler's profile screen, tap the Try button.

Test Your Brawling Skills in the Training Cave

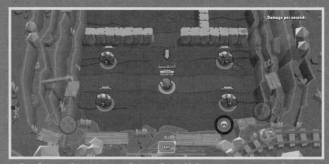

The brawler you selected will be transported to the Training Cave. Spend as much time as you want here testing out the selected brawler's Attack, Super, and Star Power capabilities as you battle against computer-controlled bots (instead of other gamers).

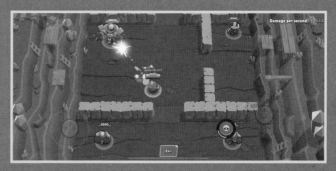

As you work your way upwards in the Training Cave, try using the Auto Aiming feature for your brawler's fighting moves. To do this, keep tapping the Fire button.

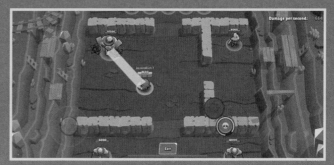

Next, be sure to practice manually aiming at your targets. You'll discover improved accuracy. To manually aim a weapon, press and hold your finger on the red weapon targeting icon, and slowly drag it in the direction you want to fire.

When aiming a weapon that shoots straight ahead, such as a gun or rifle, a white aiming line is displayed. This shows the direction you're aiming the weapon as well as the extent of its spread. If an enemy is beyond the end of the white line, they're out of range and you'll need to move closer.

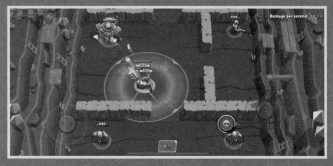

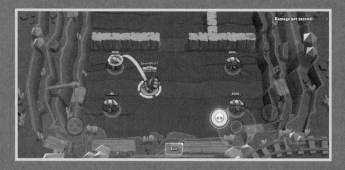

Any time you're manually aiming a throwable Attack or Super capability (such as Mama's Kiss, which is Pam's Super), as you aim it an aiming arch is displayed. Position the far end of this arch on top of your enemy or on the desired target. If the arch can't reach the desired target, it's out of range. Many throwable weapons can be tossed over (or through) a wall or solid object.

When you know your brawler's projectile weapons can be flung over walls, test this out as well, so you get good at using each available weapon in a wide range of combat situations during actual matches.

Just like in actual battles, each enemy displays a Health meter above their head. As you inflict damage on each enemy, their Health meter decreases until it gets fully depleted and the adversary is eliminated from the match. As you're becoming familiar with each brawler and testing out their skills in the Training Cave, notice how much damage you're able to inflict with each assault. A Damage Per Second score is continuously displayed in the top-right corner of the screen.

Near the top of Training Cave, you'll come across 20 bots positioned close together. Using your brawler's manual aiming capabilities and positioning your brawler in strategic locations, try to destroy multiple bots at once. Keep in mind: Many of the bots don't fight back. In an actual match, fighting enemy brawlers will be far more challenging, but the right shooting angle will allow you to cause more damage.

The bots in the Training Cave keep respawning. When you're done practicing in this area, tap the Exit button that's displayed near the bottom-center of the screen. You'll gain valuable practice here, but you won't earn Trophies or Tokens, so you won't be able to upgrade your brawlers from prizes you win by spending time here.

Consider Participating in a Friendly Game

One option for practicing in an actual arena is to participate in a Friendly Game. To do this, first select which brawler you want to control. You can only choose from the brawlers you've already unlocked. Each time you participate in a Friendly Game, all the brawlers will be fully upgraded and maxed out in terms of their capabilities.

From the Home screen, tap the Create button (located near the bottom-right corner of the screen) after selecting your favorite brawler.

From the Friendly Game screen, tap the Event button (displayed near the bottom-center of the screen) to choose the type of match you want to participate in. Be sure to scroll down to view all your options.

As you scroll down the Choose Event screen, you'll see more than a dozen Gem Grab and then Showdown Event options listed. Each takes place in a different arena.

Keep scrolling to see all the Heist Event options, as well as the Bounty Event, Brawl Ball Event, and Siege Event options, for example. Tap the one you want to experience.

Tap one Invite button at a time to see which of your online friends is available and send them an invitation.

Once you've selected an Event type, you'll be returned to the Friendly Game setup screen. Each slot displayed near the center of this screen represents one brawler who can be invited to join the match. Notice your brawler is displayed in the top-left slot, and the remaining five slots have an Invite banner below them. One at a time, invite one of your online friends to participate in the match.

*Any slots you don't fill up with personal invites to your online friends will be filled with random gamers that **Brawl Stars** automatically adds to either your team or the opposing team. Tap the Play button to kick off the match.*

A Friendly Game provides the perfect opportunity to test your brawling skills against other gamers, often while working as part of a team (depending on the Event type). This is for practice only, however. Winning matches or achieving the defined objectives during a match while playing a Friendly Game will *not* allow you to win Trophies, Tokens, Star Tokens, or any other rewards.

#2—Create Your Three-Brawler Team

Many Events in **Brawl Stars** require you to brawl with a partner or participate in a multi-brawler team. When this is the case, either have the game randomly select a partner or teammates for you or invite specific online friends to join your upcoming match (each as a partner, teammate, or adversary).

Having the game choose a random partner or teammates has some advantages and disadvantages. One advantage is that you'll potentially play with gamers whom you've never seen play before. If they're more experienced than you, you could learn new strategies and brawling techniques by following their lead during matches.

Any time **Brawl Stars** needs to randomly choose a partner or teammates for you, you'll be matched up with gamers who have a selected brawler with a similar Rank and Power Level as the brawler you've selected to control during that match. Likewise, your adversaries will all include brawlers with a similar Rank and/or Power Level. This keeps the match somewhat even.

Just because all the brawlers are evenly matched, this does not mean the gamers controlling those brawlers have equal gaming skills. Any gamer can spend many hours practicing and working with a brawler who ultimately earns a high Rank and Power Level. That gamer can then unlock a new brawler (whose Rank and Power Level will be at one, for example). Thus, while the selected brawler's fighting capabilities have not yet been upgraded, the gamer can use the strategies he's learned working with other brawlers and against many other opponents. In other words, they'll benefit from their overall brawling experience.

If you want to really put your gaming skills to the test, before a match, select your highest-ranked brawler, with the highest Power Level. You'll be placed in matches with other powerful brawlers who are likely being controlled by experienced gamers.

However, when you want to take it a bit easy and not have to work as hard to win matches or earn Trophies and Tokens, consider choosing one of your lowest-ranked brawlers (who also has a low Power Level).

When playing matches in which you're randomly partnered or matched up with teammates, it's common for two or even three gamers to be controlling a different version of the same brawler. However, when you select your own partner or teammates, each person needs to choose a different brawler to control, and each should be able to work nicely with the others to create a well-balanced team.

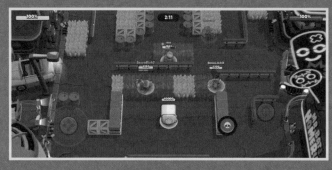

In situations when you're choosing your partner or teammates, you can choose the gamer(s) you'll play with. Each gamer chooses which brawler they want to control. Focus on choosing brawlers who work well together on a team. For example, an ideal team might include a long-range brawler, a close-range brawler, and a healer. Then, depending on the objectives of a particular Event, assign roles or tasks to each teammate, based on their brawler's skill set and the experience of the gamer controlling them.

When playing Gem Grab, you might assign the Healer to be the Gem collector. This brawler will stay near the area from where the Gems spawn. The long-range fighter might be put in charge of defeating as many enemies as possible while staying on the offense during the entire match. The close-range fighter on the team will help guard the Gem collector and defend the home turf when necessary.

During a Heist Event, the Healer could be put in charge of guarding the team's safe, while the close-range and long-range brawlers go on the offensive to destroy the enemy team's safe. Based on the type of Event you're about to experience, assign roles for each brawler on the team that make sense based on their skill set and unique capabilities.

Learning to put together well-rounded teams and then working together with your teammates to exploit each brawler's unique capabilities is one of the core skills you'll want to master if you plan to become an expert *Brawl Stars* gamer who is able to unlock all of the available brawlers and then upgrade them to their maximum Rank (20) and maximum Power Level (level 10).

Once you've manually chosen your team, prior to a match, use the Team Chat feature to discuss potential strategies with your teammates and assign roles to each brawler on the team.

Brawler Power Level Upgrade Chart

Use the following chart to help you determine when a brawler will be able to reach a specific Power Level. Keep in mind that if Supercell tweaks the game, these numbers could vary slightly in the future.

Power Level	Power Points Required	Coins Required
1	None	None
2	20	20
3	30	35
4	50	75
5	80	140
6	130	290
7	210	480
8	340	800
9*	550	1250
10**	Found in Brawl Box	2000 (Optional)

*Once a brawler reaches Power Level 9, their Star Power capabilities can be unlocked. This makes that brawler much more powerful during a brawl, especially once you've mastered how to use that brawler's Attack, Super, and Star Power capabilities.

**After your brawler reaches Power Level 9, what's required to upgrade to Power Level 10 can only be found in a box or purchased for 2,000 Coins from the Shop.

*In addition to joining Clubs to meet gamers to play with and compete against, **Brawl Stars** allows you to have up to 200 online friends. Once you join Clubs, invite members to be your friend. The game will recommend Clubs for you to join based on your Rank and accomplishments thus far in the game.*

#3—Use Gems to Buy a Token Doubler

One of the items you can buy in the Shop (using real money) is a Token Doubler (price: 50 Gems). As its name suggests, each time you participate in a match and win Tokens, that prize doubles automatically. This power-up can sometimes be won in other ways, such as by opening a Brawl Box, Big Box, or Mega Box. The more Tokens you earn, the more Brawl Boxes you can open and the faster you'll be able to upgrade your favorite brawlers.

#4—Use Your Attack (Ammo) Wisely

The Attack capability of most brawlers offers three shots at a time before it needs to recharge. This is indicated by a meter displaying three orange slots below a brawler's Health meter. Use those shots wisely. If you use up all three shots and don't defeat your target, once your brawler becomes vulnerable you can bet the enemy will come after you. Be ready to retreat, and if you can, hide in a bush until some or all of your Attack capability is replenished. Don't rely on your Health meter to keep you alive as you receive direct attacks waiting for your Attack capability to recharge.

When using manual aiming, if you don't have a good shot available, don't waste the ammo. Use the aimer to determine when you're in range and wait for the most opportune time to fire your brawler's weapon, especially when you're at mid- to long range from them. At close range, there's little need to manually aim your brawler's Attack capability. Just face the enemy and attack.

#5—Don't Walk in a Straight Line

As you're controlling your brawler during a match, have them travel in a zigzag or unpredictable pattern. Make sudden turns, change travel directions, and be as unpredictable as possible. If you simply travel in a straight line, this makes it much easier for an enemy to accurately aim at you.

Another way you can make your brawler act randomly is to constantly switch between using one, two, or three Attack capabilities in a row. If an enemy can quickly determine that every time you attack, you're going to shoot all three of your brawler's available shots, they can plan for and counteract those attacks more easily. If they can't figure out when you're going to use your brawler's Attack or how many shots they can expect, this makes it harder for them to protect themselves.

#6—Heal Up Before Your Next Attack

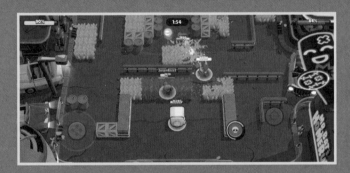

If you've taken a lot of damage, don't just wait for your Attack capability to recharge and then keep firing as soon as just one shot again becomes available. You're often better off stepping back and waiting for your Health meter to replenish and for your Attack capability to fully recharge before facing your next adversary. Remember, your brawler can't heal (their Health meter can't replenish) while you're shooting. You can see a brawler healing themselves in a bush near the center of the screen.

#7—Always Check the Bushes

Brawlers can typically not be seen while hiding in bushes! Unless you're working with a healer, the fastest way to replenish your brawler's Health is to hide in a bush. This is something your opponents will definitely do as well. Most arenas contain bushes. If you know an enemy is nearby but you can't find them, shoot one shot of your weapon into nearby bushes and see if you can weed them out. If you're controlling a brawler that specializes in close-range combat, initially launch just one Attack into a bush.

Normally, when your brawler is hiding in a bush, they can go unseen indefinitely. That is, unless an enemy steps into the same bush and walks into your brawler or very close to them, or your brawler gets hit by an attack from an enemy aiming into nearby bushes to weed out hiding brawlers.

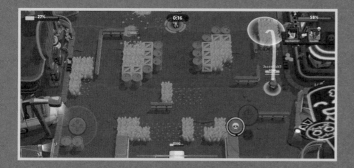

If you're about to enter into a bush to take refuge from a battle for a few seconds, there could already be an enemy hiding there. Just before entering, fire one shot into that bush. Make sure the area is clear and that you're not walking into an ambush. Shown here, JasonRich7, the gamer controlling Wizard Barley, is launching one Attack into a bush near the top-right corner of the screen to see if anyone is hiding there.

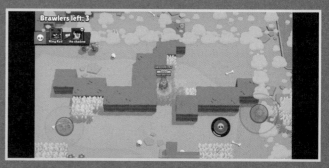

When playing a Showdown event, one strategy is to start the match by smashing crates that contain Gems, and then simply hide in a bush while several of the enemies eliminate each other. Once one or two teams are forced out of the match, your odds of winning improve. Placing third or better ensures you gain Trophies, not lose them.

If you're controlling the brawler hiding in a bush (which is called Bush Camping) and an enemy comes too close or shoots into the bush, your hiding spot will be revealed. Be prepared to protect your brawler or make a quick retreat.

#8—Look for Choke Points in Each Arena

Many arenas have very long and narrow areas brawlers need to travel through in order to reach a popular or required location. One way to defeat enemies is to wait for them to enter a choke point area. Once they're stuck in it, begin using your brawler's Attack capability. If you're working with a teammate, create surprise ambushes in and around chokeholds. Perhaps position your brawler on one end of the chokehold and your teammate or partner on the other, then attack from two directions at once.

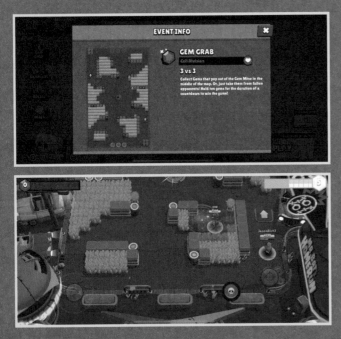

Study the arena map before a match and look for potential choke points you'll be able to exploit. Two in this arena can be found in the top-left and bottom-right corners of the map.

#9—Every Brawler's Attack Has a Range and a Spread

The weapons or fighting tools used by every brawler has both a range and a spread. The range is how far their Attack capability can travel or reach, and the spread is the width of terrain the attack can cover as the ammo, for example, spreads out. Knowing the range and spread of your own brawler's Attack capability will help you position them in the ideal spot to launch attacks. Meanwhile, knowing the capabilities of your enemies will help you keep your brawler out of harm's way. You'll know how far to stay from an enemy in order to remain safe (out of their range) and be able to dodge their attacks.

Shown here is an example of a weapon with a narrow spread but long-range capability.

Here's an example of a weapon with a long range as well as a wide spread.

Every arena is made up of tiles, a bunch of squares. A close-range weapon or attack may only be able to reach across one tile, while a projectile weapon thrown or shot might be able to cover five or six tiles.

#10—Choose Your Brawler Based on the Event and Arena

Once you choose which Event you want to participate in, determine which arena you'll be using. Each arena has a different layout and design. Some arenas are better suited for close-range brawlers, while others give long-range brawlers a tactical advantage. Be sure to choose the right brawler to control based on the challenges you anticipate encountering. Maps that are open and have fewer solid walls and obstacles are better suited to long-range brawlers, for example. Close-range brawlers tend to do better in arenas with lots of walls, solid objects, narrow passageways, and sharp turns.

*Go online and visit a free brawler ranking website, such as GameWith.net (https://gamewith.net/ brawlstars/article/show/2145), that ranks which brawlers are best suited for each specific type of Event and arena. This information changes each time Supercell makes tweaks to the game, so make sure you're using up-to-date information. Additional **Brawl Stars** resources can be found in the last section of this guide.*

#11—Be Prepared to Defend Your Teammates Even If Your Brawler Might Perish

The goal of Gem Grab is for a team of three brawlers to collect 10 Gems and hold on to them for 15 seconds to win. If one of your teammates is holding a bunch of Gems but your brawler is currently holding just a few or none, consider stepping in and protecting the brawler holding the most Gems, especially if the countdown timer is already ticking down.

Yes, your brawler might get defeated, but in this case, your team will still win and that's more important. Sometimes you need to sacrifice your brawler for the good of the team so you all benefit from receiving extra Trophies and Tokens at the end. This strategy also applies when playing a Bounty Event, for example.

Shown here, the brawler being controlled by JasonRich7 is fiercely guarding his teammate, who is currently holding 12 Gems and is hiding near the lower-left corner of the screen.

#12—Look for Arrow Tiles on the Floor of Some Arenas

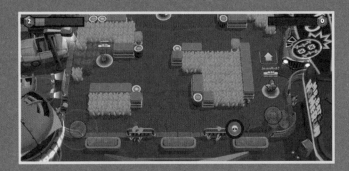

On the floor of some arenas are arrow tiles. When your brawler steps on one of these tiles, after a second or two they'll get catapulted in the direction of the arrow. This offers a faster way to reach certain areas of the arena. If you use perfect timing, these

ties can help you rush an enemy and start attacking before they realize what's happening. This is seen on the right side of the screen.

#13—Don't Get Boxed In By Water

Small bodies of water can be found throughout many arenas. Some are long and narrow, and others are L-shaped or form a zigzag pattern, for example. If you get too close to water, you'll discover your brawler typically can't cross over it. At the same time, it leaves you open to an incoming attack with nothing to hide behind. Don't allow yourself to get boxed in by an enemy, where your back is to water so you can't retreat, and one or more enemies attack from the front or the sides. Whenever possible, keep at least one tile's worth of distance between your brawler and water. In this case, the toxic green clouds that appear during a Solo Showdown match are quickly closing in and will soon trap this brawler, whose back is against a body of water.

#14—Understand the Difference Between Power Level and Rank

Any time the Home screen is displayed, your selected brawler is showcased in the center, and above their head a banner showcases their Rank and Power Level.

The brawler's Power Level is an indication of the amount of Health a brawler can have, along with how much damage they can cause using their Attack, Super, and Star Power capabilities. As you participate in matches, you'll be able to power up your brawler using Power Points, mainly found in boxes or purchased in brawler-specific bundles from the Shop. Ideally you want each of your brawlers to reach Power Level 9 so you can unlock their Star Power capabilities.

Some of the milestones you're able to reach along Trophy Road allow you to unlock bundles of Power Points that can be assigned to any unlocked brawler that you choose. Shown here, 25 Power Points that can be applied to the brawler of the

gamer's choice are about to be collected as a result of reaching the 200-Trophy milestone.

Rank is based on the number of Trophies collected using that specific brawler. A brawler's Rank is maxed out once they're used to collect 500 Trophies. These Trophies can be won during any combination of Events. Rank simply shows off how many Trophies you've won while controlling that brawler. It does not impact a brawler's offensive or defensive capabilities, like their Power Level does.

#15—Unlock and Experience Multiple Events Each Day

Each day, you'll have the opportunity to unlock different Events. Just tapping each New Event button on the Choose Event screen allows you to collect a few Tokens. However, winning a match in the newly unlocked Event will earn you one Star Token.

Redeeming 10 Star Tokens allows you to open one Big Box and increases your chances of unlocking additional brawlers. Each time a New Event becomes available, unlock it and then play it until you win one match to get that Star Token.

Each time you unlock the Ticket Event on weekends, you'll receive two bonus Tickets.

Participating in a Ticket Event typically has a one-Ticket entrance fee.

When viewing the Choose Event screen, each type of Event has its own banner. If you see a Star Power icon in the top-left corner of an Event banner, this means that if you select that Event and win, you'll earn a Star Token. Displayed in the top-right corner of each Event banner is a timer that tells you when that Event will reset and give you the opportunity to open a new Event. Shown here, the Gem Grab, Heist, and Brawl Ball Events each have a Star Token available.

#16—Use the Solo Showdown Event to Gain Trophies

If you're a newb, one easy way to upgrade your newly unlocked brawlers is to select the Solo Showdown Event and then just stick to the edges of the arena and hide in a bush while your enemies defeat each other.

Placing first, second, third, or fourth in a Showdown match, you're guaranteed to win Trophies. If you use this strategy, when the area near you is clear, smash open some boxes. Otherwise stay put until near the end of the match. Then, if you want those extra Trophies, try to beat the final one or two enemies who remain so you wind up in first place.

Only six brawlers remain in this Showdown match. The Brawler JasonRich7 is controlling is simply Bush Camping while other brawlers fight amongst themselves.

Having had to move to a different bush as the toxic green clouds moved in, the brawler being controlled by JasonRich7 (near the center of the screen) continues to be safe. Only four brawlers remain in the Showdown match.

With no brawling required and plenty of Bush Camping, this brawler earned six Trophies and ranked third in the match.

A more aggressive strategy as you improve your gaming skills is to select the Solo Showdown Event and, at the start of each match, make your way to the center of the arena and protect your position. Smash as many boxes as possible, but try to refrain to engaging enemies—at least until the end of the match. Again, if you're able to place first, second, third, or fourth, you're guaranteed to walk away with Trophies.

#17—Peek Out from Behind Walls to Lure Your Enemies

While you're safely hiding behind a wall, any time an enemy approaches, peek out for a moment so your brawler is seen. Assuming the opponent does not have a weapon that can penetrate walls, get the enemy to fire at you and waste their shots. As you see the incoming attacks, simply duck back behind the wall. Try to get your enemies to waste as much of their ammo as possible. Once the enemy needs to recharge their Attack capability, come out from behind the wall and launch your own aggressive attack on that temporarily vulnerable enemy brawler.

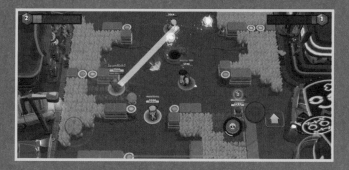

If you're controlling a brawler with a long-range weapon, another strategy that requires good aim and timing is to hide behind a wall, peek out when an enemy is approaching, fire one shot, and then duck back behind the wall for protection to avoid

any incoming shots. Keep doing this as an enemy approaches. If there's time, shoot two or even three shots in a row before retreating back behind the wall. Obviously, this strategy works best when you're attacking an enemy whose weapon(s) can't penetrate or shoot over a wall, or when attacking a brawler from a distance who has close-range capabilities and is not in range to fight back.

#18—Move In to Attack and Then Quickly Retreat

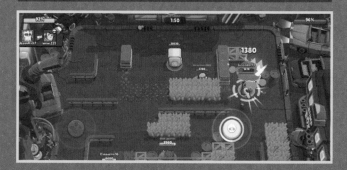

When controlling almost any of the brawlers, the closer you are to your enemy, the more damage their Attack capability can cause. (As you learned from Section 3—Meet the Brawlers, there are exceptions to this.) To maximize damage during an attack, move in, launch your attack, and then quickly retreat to put distance between you and your opponent if they haven't yet been defeated. With just a few exceptions, the distance you add will lessen the damage the enemy can inflict on you, plus it gives your own Attack time to recharge. Achieving perfect timing will take practice, especially if you use manual aiming to target your attacks more accurately.

Any time an enemy is chasing you, instead of rushing the opponent, continuously move away while shooting in their direction. They will be moving toward your incoming attack, but if they shoot back, you'll be simultaneously moving away from them and maintaining distance.

#19—Learn to Dance

To avoid incoming attacks, many gamers make their brawler quickly move from side to side in what becomes a predictable pattern. When you notice this happening, mimic the enemy's timing and movements while you're shooting. This is referred to as "dancing" and it's an effective way to win brawls against one enemy at a time. Be observant of your enemy's movements and focus on achieving perfect timing so your movements synchronize and your attacks hit their target.

#20—Gang Up On One Enemy

Any time you're playing with a partner or teammates you know well, focus on cornering a single enemy and working together to gang up on them with your attacks. If the enemy has their back to a wall or a body of water and can't retreat, and you've created a 2v1 or 3v1 scenario, guess who is most likely to win that brawl? For this strategy to work, find an area on the map where you can easily trap an enemy. Lure the enemy into that location, and

then have your partner or teammate(s) help you box them in while attacking.

If you and your partner/teammate both have long-range weapons, you can gang up on an enemy by attacking from two different sides even if you don't box them into a specific area. When the incoming attacks are from different angles, it's difficult to avoid them. For this to work, your partner or teammate needs to be on hand to position themselves in the best location based on the location of the enemy. Try to single out one enemy at a time so they're outnumbered and outgunned.

#21—Attack the Enemy's Respawn Area

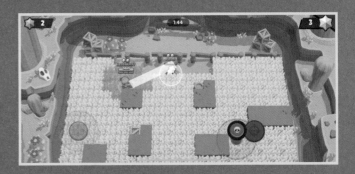

When playing 3 vs 3 Events where both teams have a respawn area, use one of your teammates to guard the opposing team's respawn area and try to keep the enemies from leaving it. Keep attacking and defeating those enemies as they respawn so they can't travel elsewhere in the arena. Meanwhile, your remaining teammate(s) can travel around the arena much more freely to achieve the Event's objectives. Using this approach, it's best to trap enemies in a corner or get them to position themselves with their back against a wall or solid object so they can't easily retreat.

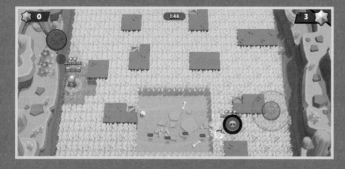

Many gamers tend to steer their brawler directly up the middle of an arena to get from one end to the other. Taking this approach, you're virtually guaranteed to encounter enemy resistance. Instead, try working your way along the right or left edge of the map—the path less taken. Shown here, Jessie is making her way up the left side of the arena.

#22—Work with Teammates and Bait Your Enemies

This strategy typically needs to be planned in advance with your partner or teammate(s). Have one ally hide in a bush so they're unseen, yet ready to attack. At the same time, another teammate can lure an enemy toward that bush. Once the enemy is close, launch a coordinated 2v1 attack to defeat that enemy brawler.

One way to lure an enemy is to make them think you're a newb or confused. Shoot one or two shots in a random direction, or have your brawler look like they're lost. An observant enemy will be drawn toward what they perceive to be an easy win, but you and your teammate will have other plans for them.

#23—Sneak Up From Behind

By hiding behind a wall or in a bush, figure out the easiest way to get behind your enemy so they have their back to you. This is an ideal time to launch an attack. You're almost guaranteed to achieve at least one or two direct hits before the enemy will have time to turn around and return fire. Be prepared to take cover and avoid those incoming attacks.

Any time you can attack an enemy that doesn't initially see you approaching, this puts you at a temporary tactical advantage. Try to attack from behind, when an enemy is not facing your brawler. Shown here, Pam is on the offensive, shooting an enemy who is running away. This also works well when confronting a Boss during a Ticketed Event.

#24—Keep Opening Boxes

The best way to upgrade your brawlers and advance through *Brawl Stars* is by unlocking and opening boxes—*without* spending a fortune to purchase them. Winning as many Trophies as you can and working your way along Trophy Road will also help you unlock brawlers, upgrade your brawlers, and obtain additional boxes.

Buying a Mega Box from the Shop can be a good investment. Check out the haul received upon opening this one.

Every day, the Shop offers a free reward. Visit the Shop daily, even if you don't plan to stick around and play **Brawl Stars**. Simply open the random reward. On this day, a 5 Power Point bundle for Carl was offered.

Just after visiting the Shop to get your free reward, check out the Choose Event screen and unlock each new Event that's become available. You'll receive 10 free Tokens just for unlocking the Event, even if you don't plan to participate in it. (As you know, 100 Tokens can be redeemed for one Brawl Box. The reward for unlocking a Ticketed Event is two Tickets, not 10 Tokens.)

Above the Play button on the Home screen, the number of Tokens available to you and that can be won at the current time is displayed. In this case, it's 200 Tokens (shown here on an iPad). After you earn the maximum number of Tokens for that time period, you can still play and win matches, but you won't receive Tokens for your efforts. The timer displayed in the top-right corner of the Play button will tell you when additional Tokens will be available. It's better to win both Trophies and Tokens for your victories during matches, as opposed to just Trophies.

#25—Ticketed Events Usually Offer the Best Prizes

Unlock the ability to participate in Ticketed Events by collecting 350 Trophies, then join one of these matches.

Each time you want to join one Ticketed Event, it will cost you one red Ticket.

Tickets can be collected for free one or two at a time. However, bundles of Tickets can be purchased from the Shop using Gems (which cost real money). Shown on the left side of the screen, the Special Offer was for 30 Tickets for the discounted price of 29 Gems (which is less than $1.99 US).

Ticketed Events are more difficult to win, but the prizes offered for winning are significant! Until you've perfected your gaming skills, don't spend money on Tickets. Take advantage of the free Tickets you receive. After you're able to win Ticketed Events consistently using your free Tickets, consider spending Gems to buy more Tickets so you can win better prizes more frequently.

Some Ticket Events involve you joining a team of three brawlers to fight one Boss and some of his computer-controlled bots. The Boss is an oversize robot with a very large Health meter (which starts out at 250,000HP and goes up from there), so it'll take a lot to defeat him. The more times you win one of these matches, the harder it'll be to defeat the Boss.

During each Ticketed Event, if you're fighting a Boss, he'll go through some changes at pre-determined time intervals. As a result of each change, he gets a little more annoyed and starts fighting back a bit harder and faster. As time goes on during a match, the bots also get harder to defeat and can cause more damage per successful attack. The more quickly your team can defeat the boss, the better!

When the Boss starts to flash and turns red, this means he's about to charge and attack. You want to dodge these attacks, so when the flashing begins, run! The laser beam attacks the Boss uses cause a lot of damage fast. Try to learn his movement and attack patterns so you can avoid them.

Attacking the Boss from behind allows you to land your attacks and stay safer than being directly in front of him. It tends to be easier to defeat the boss if your team is comprised of two close-range brawlers, such as Pam and Bull, as well as one long-range brawler, such as Colt. Working with brawlers who have their Star Power capabilities definitely makes winning these matches easier.

One reason to have Bull on your team when fighting a Boss is that he can charge. This is useful to launch attacks, but if one or more of your teammates gets eliminated, Bull can get around the arena faster to avoid bot attacks and stall until his teammates respawn. Keep in mind: during the later stages of a match, the Boss will blast away walls and solid objects, so there will be fewer places to hide.

#26—Learn to Dodge Incoming Attacks

The easiest way to dodge attacks is to understand the type of attack(s) you can expect from each type of brawler. If you're up against a long-range fighter, keep your distance unless you're rushing them to launch your own close-range attack, then move back out again. When you're at a distance, you can see the attacks approaching and quickly move out of harm's way or duck behind a wall. When you're encountering a close-range brawler, the easiest way to avoid their attacks is to not allow them to get too close. Knowing your enemy will help you stay safe.

By avoiding incoming attacks, you'll also prevent the opposing brawler to recharge their Super capability, which can only recharge when successful Attacks are launched, and they hit their target(s).

By manually aiming your own brawler's Attacks, you have a better chance of hitting your target consistently, which means your brawler's Super capability will recharge faster.

#27—Don't Stay Too Close to Your Teammates

It's a common strategy for two or three brawlers working together to stay very close together during a match. While you want to protect each other and potentially work together to launch 2v1 or 3v1 attacks against your enemies, it's not a good idea to stay too close together. Some brawler Attack capabilities have a wide spread. In other words, the ammo spreads out and can cover more area with each shot. As a result, multiple targets can be hit at the same time if those targets are standing too close together. The arena is pretty large, so spread out.

For some types of matches when your team needs to work its way from the bottom of the arena to the top, one team member should stay to the right side of the arena while one stays to the left side and the third travels up the middle. When playing a Gem Grab Event, make the brawler in the middle the Gem grabber.

#28—Be Smart When Using Your Brawler's Super Capability

The best time to use your brawler's Super capability is when you know it can impact multiple brawlers at the same time. If the Super you're working with is a weapon, wait for more than one enemy to get in range before using it. When the Super is used to heal or help your teammates, make sure they're nearby so you don't waste it.

#29—Protect Your Stars or Gems

In an Event like Gem Grab when the goal is to collect 10 or more Gems and your brawler has amassed a small collection, protect those Gems and don't get cocky. While holding a bunch of Gems, if you attack an enemy and lose, you'll lose those Gems and your brawler will need to respawn. This will be detrimental to your team's success. As a general rule, once you collect at least four Gems, be less aggressive and more defensive as you focus on protecting what you have. This also applies to Events, like Bounty, when you need to collect Stars.

#30—Keep Your Team's Healer In the Middle

One of the main responsibilities of a healer like Poco, Pam, or even Gene is to heal their teammates during team- or partner-oriented Events. During team Events, the healer should try to maintain a position near the middle of the arena or between their two teammates so those allies are easier and quicker to reach when they need healing. A healer who is too far away and can't reach their teammate(s) quickly can't perform their primary task.

During this Bounty Event, Pam's Super has been activated and in the green healing circle she's created within the arena, all her teammates are currently getting a Health boost. The team with Pam providing her healing services has collected 31 Stars, while the opposing team has just 4. Only 16 seconds remain in the match.

#31—Screenshot and Print the Arena Maps

It takes time to learn the layout of every arena. During a match, you can only see the small section of the arena you're in. To see a broader arena overview and be able to refer to it during matches, follow these steps:

Step #1—Start at the Home screen and tap the Event button.

Step #2—Instead of tapping the center of an unlocked Event, tap the Info ("i") button displayed in the top-right corner of the Event's oversized button.

Step #3—When you see the Event Info screen with an overview of the arena map displayed in the right side, take a screenshot. Using the Photos app, select the screenshot and print it out.

Step #4—During a match in that arena, refer to the printout as needed to discover where the walls, bushes, bodies of water, and bottlenecks are located. Choose the best route to where you want to go, or use the map to find hiding spots or locations from which you can launch attacks, for example. After you've played a few matches in each arena you'll probably memorize the layout, but until then, having a printout of the entire arena to refer to during a match will be helpful.

A Selection of Arena Layouts

The following are a sampling of eight arena layouts, including arenas from Gem Grab, Showdown, Heist, Bounty, Brawl Ball, and Siege Events.

The Hard Rock Mine arena from a Gem Grab Event.

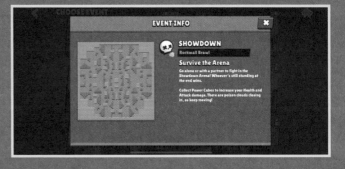

The Rockwall Brawl arena from a Showdown Event.

The Kaboom Canyon arena from a Heist Event.

The Temple Ruins arena from a Bounty Event.

The Excel arena from a Bounty Event.

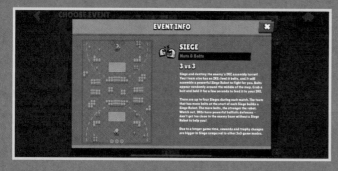

The Nuts & Bolts arena from a Siege Event.

The Super Stadium arena from a Brawl Ball Event.

The Hunting Party arena from the Big Game Ticket Event.

#32—Blast Away Solid Barriers When Necessary

Depending on which brawler you're controlling, if they have a long-range weapon that can't travel over or through walls or solid barriers, you might want to destroy the solid objects in your path. This leaves fewer places to hide and avoid incoming attacks, but it also makes close-range brawlers more vulnerable because you'll be able to see them approaching from farther away and can attack them before they're close enough to reach you.

Not all brawlers have the ability to destroy walls and solid objects, so this might be a situation when you'll need to work in conjunction with your teammates and pre-plan your overall strategy before the match kicks off.

#33—Avoid the Toxic Green Clouds

During certain types of Events, after a match begins, toxic green clouds form around the edges of the arena and slowly expand inward. This drives the surviving brawlers toward the center of the arena and closer together, so they're basically forced to brawl. If your plan is to Bush Camp until some of your enemies defeat each other, keep an eye on the toxic clouds. You may need to periodically move to avoid them. If you time your moves correctly, when no enemies are in sight, you should be able to remain unseen until the late stages of the match when only two or three brawlers remain. Stay alive as long as possible, even if you need to brawl to win the most Trophies possible.

Bush Camping closer to the center of the arena will allow you to avoid the toxic clouds longer while remaining unseen. Some of your brawler's Health will get depleted for every second they get caught inside a toxic cloud, so it's best to avoid them. While one or two seconds' worth of contact is easy to recover from once you leave the toxic cloud, anything longer could cause your brawler to get eliminated from the match or force them to walk directly into an enemy's attack if they've waited too long to escape the cloud.

#34—Choose Any Event and Arena Map When Playing a Friendly Game

In addition to allowing you to practice working with specific brawlers, and being able to choose your teammates and your adversaries from your online friends (unless you choose to play with random gamers), playing a Friendly Game allows you to pick from any of the *Brawl Stars* Events, plus select which arena you want to play in. This allows you to preview Events and arenas that you haven't yet been able to unlock by playing normal matches.

#35—Support Your Teammates in Gem Grab

Gem Grab is just one of the Events in which you're required to be part of a three-brawler team.

If you're more interested in brawling than grabbing Gems, choose a brawler with a long-range weapon and then position that brawler within targeting distance of the Gem Spawning location. If possible, hide in a bush. As enemy brawlers approach the Gem spawning location, launch attacks. Once you defeat them, they'll drop the Gem(s) they're carrying, allowing one of your teammates to pick them up. Meanwhile, keep your distance and continue to protect the turf as the other brawler(s) on your team assigned to be the Gem Collector grab the Gems.

After the Gem Collector on your team has acquired five or more Gems, they should retreat and hide to protect the Gems in their possession. Allow another teammate to collect the rest of the required Gems. Once your team has 10 Gems, don't get greedy or cocky. Protect what you have for the required 15 seconds to win the match. If you continue brawling while holding Gems and get defeated, your team will forfeit those Gems and they'll need to be reclaimed. This strategy also works when playing a Heist or Bounty Event.

SECTION 5

WHAT'S OFFERED FROM THE SHOP

One of the ways you can advance to higher levels in **Brawl Stars**, as well as unlock and upgrade your brawlers is by making in-game purchases from the Shop. You'll need to use real money to purchase green Gems, and then redeem those Gems for various items, including skins that will alter the appearance of your favorite brawlers.

To access the Shop, from the Home screen, tap the Shop icon that's displayed near the top-left corner of the screen.

Check Out the Daily Deals

Each day, the Shop presents a Special Offer. It's displayed on the left side of the screen. This might be the opportunity to purchase a bundle of Power Points, Tickets, or Gems at a discounted price. Shown here, a 220 Power Point bundle that could be applied to any brawler was offered for 39 Gems (which equates to about $3 US).

By scrolling to the right while visiting the Shop, you'll see a Daily Deals heading. These offers change every day. There's always a free item being offered in the top-right slot of the Daily Deals sections, so be sure to visit the Shop daily to redeem it.

Also below the Daily Deals heading you'll discover bundles of Power Points being offered that can be applied to specific brawlers. These items can typically be redeemed using Coins,

not Gems. As you unlock brawlers and collect coins, visit the Shop and use Coins to acquire Power Points for your brawlers so you can upgrade their Power Level.

On a typical day, the Shop will have four different Power Point bundles, but these offers change daily. Remember, it's a good strategy to upgrade all your unlocked brawlers as evenly as possible, as opposed to putting all of your efforts into maximizing just one brawler's capabilities.

How to Upgrade a Brawler Using Power Points

After winning Power Points or purchasing them, to upgrade your brawler(s), exit out of the Shop, return to the Home screen, and then tap the Brawlers icon (displayed below the Shop icon, on the left side of the screen).

One way to unlock brawlers is to look for a slot under the Daily Deals heading that allows you to purchase a random brawler in a specific rarity category for a fixed price. For the price of 350 Gems, a special offer for a random Mythic brawler was offered in the Shop. Upon making the purchase, the brawler who was unlocked was none other than Tara.

When a brawler's Power Level can be upgraded, you'll see a green Upgrade banner below that brawler's slot. As you can see here, Darryl can be upgraded.

From the bottom-right corner of El Primo's Info screen, you can see he can be upgraded to Power Level 7 by purchasing the upgrade for 480 Coins. The higher the Power Level you're upgrading to, the more Coins it'll cost once you've collected enough Power Points.

Tap the Price icon once to see how that brawler's Health, Attack, and Super abilities will be impacted by upgrading to the next Power Level, then tap the now-flashing Price button again to perform the upgrade and spend the required Coins.

Big Boxes and Mega Boxes Can Be Purchased As Well

Tokens are used to acquire and open Brawl Boxes. You'll earn Tokens by winning matches or achieving specific objectives during Events. Big Boxes can be acquired and opened by collecting 10 Star Tokens. However, from the Shop, it's always possible to purchase a Big Box for 30 Gems or a Mega Box for 80 Gems. Sometimes a special discount is offered, so be on the lookout for those offers.

To discover the probability of receiving specific rewards, from the Shop, tap either the Big Box or Mega Box slot once. A Confirm Purchase window will pop up on the screen (shown here). Tap the Info ("i") icon that's displayed in the top-left corner of this window.

The Big Box Info or Mega Box Info screen explains what you could receive by opening that box. The probability of receiving: Power Points + Coins, unlocking a Rare brawler, unlocking a Super Rare brawler, unlocking an Epic brawler, unlocking a Mythic brawler, unlocking a Legendary brawler, or unlocking Star Power is displayed.

Only tap the green Price button on the Confirm Purchase screen if you want to spend Gems to open the displayed box.

Skins Can be Purchased Using Star Points

Scroll to the right while visiting the Shop. Below the heading that says Star Shop, you'll see special offers for exclusive skins for specific brawlers that can only be acquired by redeeming Star Points. The selection of skins offered in the Star Shop section changes daily.

Consider Purchasing a Token Doubler

By spending 50 Gems, you can purchase a Token Doubler. In this case, for the next 1,000 Tokens you win by participating in Events, your winnings will automatically be doubled. This means you'll be able to buy more Brawl Boxes faster because you'll be able to collect twice the number of Tokens for a specific amount of time.

Ultimately, the items you receive from Brawl Boxes, Big Boxes, or Mega Boxes could include new brawlers, brawler skins, bundles of Power Points for specific brawlers, bundles of Tokens, bundles of Coins, or bundles of Tickets. The more boxes you open, the better your chances will be of unlocking new brawlers

without having to pay for them or wait until you acquire enough Tokens to unlock them from Trophy Road.

The Shop Sells Gem Packs

As you scroll to the right in the Shop, you'll see the Gem Packs heading. It contains six slots, each of which offers a different size bundle of green Gems you can purchase using real money. The larger the bundle you purchase, the bigger the discount you receive.

The Price of Gem Packs

Number of Gems	Price of the Gem Pack (US Dollars)
30	$1.99
80	$4.99
170	$9.99
360	$19.99
950	$49.99
2,000	$99.99

Always check the Special Offers section on the left side of the Shop screen for discounted Gem bundles. Also, each time you open a Brawl Box, for example, you could randomly receive a few Gems as a bonus.

Use Gems to Purchase Coin Bundles

Using Gems, it's also possible to purchase bundles of Coins. These are called Coin Packs in the Shop. Coins can then be used to purchase Power Point bundles from the Shop. For 20 Gems, you're able to purchase 150 Coins. Using 50 Gems, purchase 400 Coins. The cost of 1,200 Coins is 140 Gems.

Quit Shopping and Start Brawling

To exit the Shop, either tap the Home icon displayed in the top-right corner of the Shop, or tap the "<" icon displayed in the top-left corner.

Displayed along the top of the screen, no matter what you're doing in the game, is the number of Star Points, Coins, and Gems you currently have available. Once you unlock Ticket Events and begin collecting or purchasing Tickets, the number of Tickets you currently have available is also displayed near the top of the screen, as you can see here.

Redeem Prizes From Trophy Road

From the Home screen, tap the Trophy counter displayed below your name in the top-left corner of the screen to access Trophy Road.

On the Home screen, when the Trophy Road banner on the Home screen changes to yellow (with a red and white star icon), this indicates a new milestone has been reached and is ready to be unlocked.

As you win Trophies by participating in Events, your total number of Trophies based on each of the unlocked brawlers you control during matches helps you progress along Trophy Road (shown here). When you reach a specific milestone that's listed, you'll receive the displayed prize.

The following chart shows you the eight brawlers that can be unlocked for free once you achieve specific milestones along Trophy Road:

*In the future, as additional brawlers are introduced into **Brawl Stars** by Supercell, some of them may become unlockable from Trophy Road.

Number of Trophies Required	Brawler Who Gets Unlocked*
10	Nita
60	Colt
250	Bull
500	Jessie
1,000	Brock
2,000	Dynamike
3,000	Bo
4,000	Tick

Shown here, Jessie is about to be unlocked along Trophy Road after collecting 500 Trophies. Other prizes available for reaching specific milestones along Trophy Road include Brawl Boxes, the unlocking of new Event types, additional Brawlers, Coin bundles, Power Point bundles, and other goodies.

SECTION 6

JOIN SOME ONLINE CLUBS AND CHAT

There are two ways to experience *Brawl Stars* with other gamers. First, you can have the game match you up with random players who are controlling brawlers closely matched with yours. In this case, you can't choose who you'll play with or play against, or which brawlers the other gamers will be controlling.

The second way to experience *Brawl Stars* is by choosing who you play with and/or compete against, depending on which Event you're about to experience. As you're about to discover, there are several ways to meet and interact with fellow gamers.

How to Choose Your Name

Every gamer who experiences *Brawl Stars* must set up a free online-based account, which includes creating a name. This is how people recognize you in the game. If you don't want to use your first and last name for privacy reasons, come up with a name that's unique, funny, or memorable, but that won't be offensive to others.

How to Change Your Name

After setting up your *Brawl Stars* account initially, you can change your name once for free. After that, it'll cost you 60 Gems (around $4 US) to change your name, and you'll need to wait at least three days between name changes.

To change your name in *Brawl Stars*, follow these steps:

Step #1—To access it from the Home screen, tap the Menu icon (in the top-right corner of the Home screen).

Step #2—Tap the Settings button.

Step #3—From the Settings screen, tap the Change Name button.

Step #4—When you see the Change Name pop-up for the first time, tap the Free button to change your username (for free). Otherwise, tap on the green 60 Gem button.

Step #5—Within the Enter New Name field on the Change Name screen, type the name you want to use. This is displayed publicly, so you might *not* want to use your full first and last name in order to protect your privacy. Tap the Continue button.

Step #6—Re-enter your new username when prompted.

Step #7—You'll be asked, "Are you sure you want to change your name?" Your new name will be displayed. In the field below it, type the word "CONFIRM" in all capital letters, and then tap the Okay button.

Step #8—After completing the Change Name process, you'll be returned to the Home screen. Your new Name will be displayed in the top-left corner of the screen. Moving forward, as you join matches, this is the name other gamers will see displayed in conjunction with your brawler.

Linking with Facebook

If you're already active on Facebook and have a bunch of online friends, consider linking your Facebook account with your *Brawl Stars* account.

To do this, from the Home screen, tap the Menu icon. Next, tap the Settings button, and then from the Settings screen (shown here) tap the Facebook Connect button displayed below the Friends heading. When the permission box appears, tap the Continue button. Once your two accounts are linked (which only needs to be done once), *Brawl Stars* allows you to communicate with your Facebook friends who also play *Brawl Stars* from within the game.

To see which of your Facebook and *Brawl Stars* friends are online so you can chat and/or send them an invitation, from the Home screen, tap the Social icon. At the top of the Social screen (shown here), tap the Friends tab at the top of the screen.

On the left side of the Friends screen are the Facebook Connected and LINE Connect buttons. On the right side of this screen, your Facebook friends who are online are displayed. Tap a listing to access a mini-menu that allows you to manage each friend.

Tap the Remove button to remove the friend. Tap the Spectate button to watch your online friend play the match they're currently participating in, or tap the Profile button to see their *Brawl Stars* profile.

Use LINE Connect to Link with Online Friends

When you use the Connect to LINE feature from within Settings, you're able to link your LINE account with your *Brawl Stars* account. This allows you to see your LINE friends listed in the Friends list in *Brawl Stars*, and they'll be able to see your account info and stats as well.

Once the two accounts are connected, you're also able to send your LINE friends invites.

LINE is a free communications and messaging app that has more than 600 million active users around the world. Linking your LINE account with Brawl Stars *only needs to be done once. To accomplish this, from the Home screen, tap the Menu icon. Tap the Settings button, and then tap the LINE Connect button (shown here). You must already have an active LINE account set up.*

When prompted, enter your LINE email address and password, then tap the Log In button. (If you have not already done so, tap the Install Line option to install the free LINE app onto your mobile device.)

Participate in *Brawl Stars* Clubs

Any **Brawl Stars** players can create an online club for free and accept new members into that club. It's also possible for a gamer to simply join a Club as a member, so they always have others to chat with and participate in matches with.

A Club is similar to a "clan" in other games. Someone can have one of four titles within a **Brawl Stars** Club. There is one President, one Vice President, Senior Members, and then Members. The person who creates the Club automatically becomes President. Up to 100 gamers can join a Club.

To find a Club to join, from the Home screen, tap the Social button. At the top of the Social screen (shown here), tap the Clubs tab. Based on your overall player stats, on the right side of the screen, a bunch of Clubs will be listed.

Tap any Club listing to see the Club's members and learn a bit more about it. Some Clubs are Closed or Invite Only. Under the Type heading, look for the word "Open." This indicates anyone can join by tapping the Join button. Some Clubs require you to have earned a pre-determined number of Trophies before joining. This requirement is displayed under the **Required Trophies** *heading on the left side of the screen, just above the* **Join** *button.*

To create your own Club, access the Club screen (shown here) and then tap the Create Club button. You'll be asked to create a Club Name and a brief Description for your Club. Try to come up with an original and creative name. Next, choose a Badge design by tapping the Browse button below the Badge heading. Also, select your Club Location (which should be your home country).

At the bottom of the Create a New Club screen, tap the "<" or ">" icon under the Type heading to choose whether you want your Club to be Open (meaning anyone can join), Invite Only, or Closed. (A Closed Club has the maximum number of members or does not accept new members.) Below the Required Trophies heading, tap the "<" or ">" icon to set the prerequisite number of Trophies a gamer must already have to join your Club. You'll get more random members joining your Club if you set the Type to Open.

If you want a lot of random people to join your Club quickly, as soon as it's established, get your online friends to immediately join so you join a bunch of members right from the start and the Club appears to be popular. People don't like joining Clubs that have just a few members. Another way to attract gamers to your Club is to invite all the random players you're matched up with while playing *Brawl Stars*, especially if those people turn out to be skilled.

In order to keep your Club popular, be sure to stay active in the Chat. As President, get your Vice President and Senior Members to post on a regular basis and keep the conversation flowing. Members are more apt to stay in a Club that's active and that features interesting conversations. Also make sure people stick to the rules and treat all your members in a friendly way and with respect. Posting nasty comments, or cyber bullying, or harshly critiquing someone's gaming skills should not be permitted or tolerated.

To avoid creating a Club that attracts newbs and unskilled players you'd wind up getting frustrated with if you had to play with them, set the Required Trophies to a setting that's close to how many Trophies you have amassed. To ensure you wind up with serious players as members, adjust this setting to 400 or higher. There are options between 0 and 15,000. Once you've completed the Create a New Club form,

tap the Create button to establish the Club. As you improve as a *Brawl Stars* gamer, you can always boost the Required Trophies setting for your Club.

In addition to the social aspect of joining a Club, another key benefit is that you can easily find gamers with similar stats and skills to play with or add to your team. As soon as your Club has been created, you're able to send out invitations for people to join it. Use the Share Invite feature to do this.

The Share Invite feature allows you to send a personal invitation with a direct link to your Club to anyone via text message or email. You can also create a posting to be published on Twitter or Facebook, for example.

To create a Post (a message that a Club's members can see), tap the megaphone icon on the Club Management screen, type your message, and then tap the Post button.

Participate in Team Chats

*To chat with Club members who are online, from the **Home** screen, tap the **Chat** icon (displayed near the top-right corner of the screen), and then tap the **Club Chat** tab at the top of the screen. To create a message, tap the text bubble near the bottom-right corner of the screen, type your message, and tap the **Done** button. Everyone in the Club who accesses the Chat will be able to see and respond to all messages.*

To keep up a lively and fun conversation within your Club's Chat, ask questions and encourage people to be active. Questions you can pose that'll encourage chat participation include:

- Who is your favorite brawler and why?
- What is your favorite Event type and why?
- Which arenas do you love or hate the most?
- Which is your favorite skin for [insert brawler's name]?
- If you had 5,000 free Gems, how would you spend them in the Shop?
- Who do you think are the top five best brawlers?
- Who do you think are the worst five brawlers?

- What is the longest you've spent playing *Brawl Stars* at one time? What did you accomplish during that time?
- If you could create your own brawler from scratch, what Attack, Special, and Star Power capabilities would it have? What would their name be?

You don't need to be a Club's President to strike up a conversation or chat with other players in a Club Chat. Of course, you can also invite any Club member to be your online friend and then chat with that gamer privately.

Club Chats are public forums. Make sure you don't share too much information about yourself with strangers. For example, don't give out your full name, where you live, details about what school you go to, your phone number, or any other personal information. Also, never give out your *Brawl Stars* account password to people you meet online.

Chat with Online Players

Whether or not you choose to join a Club, you always have the option to become friends with the random players you're matched up with and then chat with them (when they're your teammates) online using the Chat feature built into the *Brawl Stars* app.

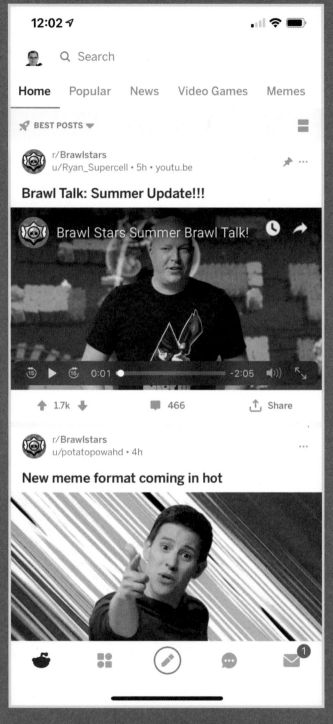

*Reddit (www.reddit.com) has an active **Brawl Stars** community that can be found at: r/Brawlstars. To access this community, visit the Reddit website, or download and install the free Reddit mobile app (shown here). Next, create a free Reddit account.*

One subgroup on Reddit (/rBrawlRecuit) is dedicated specifically to gamers looking to join a Club or recruit new members to their **Brawl Stars** Club.

Another subgroup (r/BrawlStarsCompetitive) is dedicated to sharing **Brawl Stars** strategies. Here you can post questions about **Brawl Stars** or share your own tips and strategies with other gamers in a public forum.

SECTION 7

BRAWL STARS ONLINE RESOURCES

On YouTube (www.youtube.com), Twitch.TV (www.twitch.tv), or Facebook Watch (www.facebook.com/watch), Mixer (www.mixer.com) in the Search field, enter the search phrase "*Brawl Stars*" to discover many game- related channels, livestreams, and prerecorded videos that'll help you become a better player.

*It's possible to watch livestreams of the best **Brawl Stars** players from directly within the game using the Brawl TV feature. To do this, from the Home screen, tap the menu icon that's located in the top-right corner. Tap the Brawl TV icon, and then tap the Go button when you see the message, "Spectate top-level **Brawl Stars** players from around the world." Livestreams of different Events will keep playing until you tap the Exit button. Watch and learn!*

Also, be sure to check out the following online resources related to *Brawl Stars*:

WEBSITE	DESCRIPTION	URL
Apple App Store	Download and install the iOS version of *Brawl Stars* onto your iPhone or iPad.	https://apps.apple.com/us/app/brawl-stars/id1229016807
Best Brawler Rankings from GameWith.net	Discover how each brawler ranks related to the game's various Events.	https://gamewith.net/brawlstars/article/show/2145
BlueStacks4	Use this emulator on your Windows PC or Mac to play the Android version of *Brawl Stars* on your computer.	www.bluestacks.com
Brawl Stars Blog from Supercell	Get the latest news related to *Brawl Stars* from the game developer's official blog.	www.brawlstars.com
Brawl Stars Community on Discord	Join the *Brawl Stars* community on Discord and chat with its more than 50,000 members.	https://discordapp.com/invite/brawlstars

WEBSITE	DESCRIPTION	URL
Brawl Stars Daily (BSD)	Check out this independent website that offers news, strategies, and other content related exclusively to **Brawl Stars**.	www.brawlstarsdaily.com
Brawl Stars Leaderboards	See a real-time list of the top-ranked **Brawl Stars** players and Clubs around the world.	Launch **Brawl Stars**. From the game screen, tap the **Menu** icon. Tap the **Leaderboards** button. Tap a specific listing to see that player or Club's stats.
Brawl Stars News	This independent website offers strategies, forums, and news related to **Brawl Stars**.	www.brawlstarsnews.com
Brawl Stars Social Media Links	Check out the official **Brawl Stars** YouTube channel, Facebook page, Reddit feed, Twitter feed, and Twitch channel.	**YouTube** www.youyube.com/brawlstars **Facebook** www.facebook.com/brawlstars **Reddit** www.reddit.com/r/Brawlstars **Twitter** @BrawlStars **Twitch** www.twitch.tv/brawlstars
Brawl Stats for **Brawl Stars**	This free iOS app allows you to see your personal stats, including Trophies and win/loss records, plus look up the stats for other gamers. Simply enter the gamer's tag number to see their stats or tap the Top icon to see a list of the best players and Clubs. This is an independent app that's not affiliated with Supercell.	https://apps.apple.com/us/app/brawl-stats-for-brawl-stars/id1433889837
BrawlStarsUp.com (BSU)	Discover strategies and the latest gaming info from this independent website. It covers everything related to **Brawl Stars** and gets updated often.	www.brawlstarsup.com

WEBSITE	DESCRIPTION	URL
Coach Cory—*Brawl Stars* YouTube Channel	A popular YouTube channel that covers all things having to do with *Brawl Stars.* Coach Cory's YouTube channel has more than 21 million views.	www.youtube.com/channel /UCr8T8FRUsvJ5MU9idLoYKIA
Fandom's *Brawl Stars* Wiki	Learn more about some of the more intricate aspects of the game that get updated and tweaked often by Supercell. This independent site includes free articles and videos.	www.brawlstars.fandom.com
Google Play Store	Download and install the Android version of *Brawl Stars* to your Android-based mobile device	https://play.google.com/store/apps /details?id=supercell.brawlstars
Jason R. Rich's Website	Learn more about the author of this strategy guide and learn about his many other unofficial game guides (focusing on *Fortnite: Battle Royale, PUBG, Apex Legends,* and other popular games). He's also written books covering many other topics.	www.JasonRich.com www.GameTipBooks.com Twitter: @JasonRich7 Instagram: @JasonRich7 Facebook: @JasonRich7
PocketGamer.biz	Read the latest news coverage this mobile gaming website offers about *Brawl Stars*.	www.pocketgamer.biz
Supercell's Official Website	Check out the official website of game developer Supercell to learn more about *Brawl Stars* and the company's other mobile games, including: *Clash Royale, Boom Beach,* and *Clash of Clans.*	www.supercell.com
TwitchMetrics	View a list of the current most-watched *Brawl Stars* streamers on Twitch.tv.	www.twitchmetrics.net/channels/ viewership?game=Brawl+Stars

Your Brawling Excitement and Challenges Continue . . .

One of the really awesome things about **Brawl Stars** is that it gives you the chance to unlock and control more than 27 different brawlers. By upgrading your brawlers, you make them stronger and more powerful.

At the same time, you're able to participate in several different types of Events and experience Events in different arenas. As a result, there are many different, exciting, challenging, and fun-filled gaming experiences to be had when playing **Brawl Stars** on your favorite Internet-connected mobile device.

Want something new? Supercell has your back! The company is continuously updating the game with new features, Events, arena layouts, brawlers, skins, tweaks, and other goodies, so be sure to stay up to date about what's been added to the game recently.

As a newb, don't expect instant success! **Brawl Stars** takes plenty of practice to master. The game is designed to take a lot of time for you to progress through it, so be patient and keep plugging away. If you get frustrated because you keep getting eliminated from one type of Event using a particular brawler, try changing brawlers or switch Event types.

While you may want to spend real money on in-app purchases to unlock or upgrade brawlers faster, as a newb, first focus on improving your brawling techniques with the brawlers you can unlock and control for free. Then spend your money wisely to get the best items or upgrades for the least amount of money possible. Remember, you can have countless hours of fun playing **Brawl Stars** without spending a penny!

You always have the option to play **Brawl Stars** with your online Facebook friends, plus interact with other gamers who love **Brawl Stars** as much as you. Building your own teams adds an additional strategy-related element to the game because you can pre-plan each teammate's role and coordinate offensive attacks. When choosing your teammates, focus on building well-rounded teams comprised of brawlers that work well together and complement each other's skills based on which Event you plan to experience.

No matter what approach you take when playing, your goals are to win matches, achieve the Star Player title at the end of each match, and to keep collecting Trophies and Tokens.

Good luck and have fun!